Advance Praise for *The "Perfect" Parent*

"Parenting consciously is at the heart of raising emotionally healthy children. This book offers wonderful tools to navigate the world of engaged, attuned, and conscious parenting."

—**Dr. Shefali Tsabary**, clinical psychologist and author of *The Conscious Parent*; featured on *Oprah's Lifeclass*

"*The 'Perfect' Parent* is packed with practical, easy-to-remember tips and simple strategies for establishing meaningful connections between parents and children of all ages. This book will be a huge relief for all those overwhelmed parents and maxed-out moms who want to bring out the best in themselves and their kids."

—**Dr. Christine Carter**, author of *Raising Happiness*; director of the Greater Good Parents program at UC Berkeley's Greater Good Science Center

"A wonderful, touching, thoughtful book that will help every person become the parent they hoped to be, to love, learn, communicate, connect, and feel alive in that wonderful, impossible life job, raising fine children. Every new parent should read this book; every grandparent-to-be should gift it to their children."

—**Alvin Rosenfeld, MD**, clinical professor of psychiatry at Weill Cornell Medical College; coauthor of *The Over-Scheduled Child: Avoiding the Hyper-Parenting Trap*

"Parents, you can relax! *The 'Perfect' Parent* reassures you that you can trust your child-raising instincts. It also provides you with five tools to use when you hit a rough patch."

—**David Walsh, PhD**, psychologist and author of *Why Do They Act That Way? A Survival Guide to the Adolescent Brain for You and Your Teen*

"A much-needed and timely book on the transformative nature of parenting—the key to a healthier, happier family and society."

—**The Venerable Tenzin Priyadarshi**, founding director of the Dalai Lama Center for Ethics and Transformative Values at the Massachusetts Institute of Technology

"Roma Khetarpal has created a true guidebook for all parents seekinily environment sans unnecessary guilt, doubt, and fear. For so ma become an overwhelming endeavor in our modern world. But the and that way is clearly laid out through the insights and anecdote: book. The opportunity to shift the parenting perspective and truly ent is available to all who desire it. It's time to cut through the oute in touch with the core aspects of the parent/child relationship. Th for helping us to traverse the long and winding road of parenting."

—**Annie Burnside**, award-winning author of *Soul to Soul Parenting*

"Parenting is difficult and our training is so limited. This insightful, touching, and well-written book teaches effective parenting by guiding parent-child communications. It will help improve and promote your child's growth and development."

—**Edward Farber, PhD**, author of *Raising the Kid You Love with the Ex You Hate*

"Roma Khetarpal gives parents practical tools to better understand and engage with their children."

—**Jonathan Hewitt**, author of *Life Ki-Do Parenting: Tools to Raise Happy, Confident Kids from the Inside Out*

"Roma's message of respecting children as individuals, listening to what they're saying, and understanding and controlling one's own emotions and responses is powerful."

—**Dr. Richard Cohen**, director of Project ABC Family Wellness Network, Children's Institute, Inc.

"Too many parenting books leave one feeling full of information while nagged by insecurity. Not *The 'Perfect' Parent*. With empathy, humor, and practical advice, Roma Khetarpal's words read like a conversation with a trusted friend."

—**Asha Dornfest**, coauthor of *Minimalist Parenting: Enjoy Modern Family Life More by Doing Less*; founder and editor of *Parent Hacks*

"While parenting can be a rich and rewarding activity, it is by no means an easy task. Khetarpal's *The 'Perfect' Parent* provides a novel approach to navigating the complex terrain of parenthood. Synthesizing her own experiences as a mother with current research from psychology and cognitive neuroscience, this is a valuable resource to any parent wishing to improve communication and cultivate greater empathy with their children. As a professor specializing in the neuroscience of health and happiness, I am genuinely pleased to share Khetarpal's wisdom and insights with my own community, advancing the concept that becoming the perfect parent is now a reality."

—**Dr. Jay Kumar**, author of *Brain, Body & Being*

"I truly enjoyed reading *The 'Perfect' Parent* and even have a journal for my favorite quotes. I keep it on hand for when I need a reminder on communicating better with my own children."

—**Maribel Reyes**, owner and writer at *Stroller Adventures*

"What a gift! A practical, humorous, easy-to-read, complete handbook for every parent or soon-to-be parent! Roma brings self-effacing honesty and practical tools and insight into her discussion of the importance of communication, flexibility, and trust in parenting. Accepting and respecting our children the way we would love to be accepted and respected teaches them inner strength, calmness, and kindness. In her wonderful real-life examples, she shows how spending time listening to and understanding them is time well spent. We have as much to learn from our children as we have to teach them."

—**Yvonne Oswald, PhD**, award-winning, bestselling author of *Every Word Has Power*

"*The 'Perfect' Parent* is a brilliant, easy-to-read guide that focuses on some of the most important yet rarely explored aspects of parenting, including creating loving, connected relationships with your children. By shifting the focus of parenting from discipline and completing a checklist of daily tasks to mindfully connecting with your children and yourself, you can create endless opportunities for building communication and great relationships with your kids!"

—**Leslie Anne Ross, PsyD**, vice president of the Leadership Center at
Children's Institute, Inc.

"P^{The}erfect" parent

5 Tools *for* Using Your Inner Perfection

to **Connect with Your Kids**

ROMA KHETARPAL

GREENLEAF
BOOK GROUP PRESS

Published by Greenleaf Book Group Press
Austin, Texas
www.gbgpress.com

Copyright ©2014 Roma Khetarpal

Distributed by Greenleaf Book Group LLC

For ordering information or special discounts for bulk purchases, please contact Greenleaf Book Group LLC at PO Box 91869, Austin, TX 78709, 512.891.6100.

Design and composition by Greenleaf Book Group LLC
Cover design by Greenleaf Book Group LLC

Publisher's Cataloging-In-Publication Data

Khetarpal, Roma.
   The "perfect" parent : 5 tools for using your inner perfection to connect with your kids / Roma Khetarpal.—First edition.

   pages : illustrations ; cm

   Issued also as an ebook.
   Includes bibliographical references.
   ISBN: 978-1-62634-103-6

   1. Parent and child. 2. Parenting. 3. Communication in families. 4. Child rearing. I. Title.

HQ755.85 .K44 2014
306.874   2014931325

Part of the Tree Neutral® program, which offsets the number of trees consumed in the production and printing of this book by taking proactive steps, such as planting trees in direct proportion to the number of trees used: www.treeneutral.com

Printed in the United States of America on acid-free paper

14 15 16 17 18 19   10 9 8 7 6 5 4 3 2 1

First Edition

Other Edition(s)
eBook ISBN: 978-1-62634-104-3

TreeNeutral®

Honoring . . .

My Mama and Papa—You are the first inspiration of these pages. Thank you for making every life lesson a love lesson.

My beautiful kids, Nitasha and Navin—Remember, my sweet loves, you define me and my purpose. Your only payback is to pay it forward.

And my soul mate, Harish—Your love, acknowledgment, acceptance, and encouragement of who I am and what completes me have enriched my life beyond imagination. Can we have another lifetime together? This one might not be enough.

Contents

Foreword

What do we really want for our kids—not just today (to eat their vegetables and get a good night's sleep) or even in the next few years (to learn to read and ride a bike, to be a responsible student and get into college), but for their entire life?

I believe Roma has it right, and, as you read on, I think you'll benefit from her perspective on what we truly desire for our children. I also think you'll be enlightened by her take on what we, as parents, want for ourselves out of parenting.

As a researcher, developmental psychologist, and parent, I have read many articles and books about parenting. I was an undergraduate psychology major at Stanford twenty-plus years ago, when I became interested in how kids think. I took classes, taught at a preschool, and continued my studies in developmental psychology at the University of Michigan, where I earned my PhD. I worked in the research department at Disney Cable Networks Group and later as an independent consultant. At that point I thought I knew a lot about kids. And then I had my own children, and I realized that theoretical knowledge and practical knowledge can be worlds apart. I turned my researcher's gaze on parenting and read how-to books as though I was preparing for final exams!

Over the years as my two sons have grown from infants to toddlers to grade-schoolers, I have developed quite a collection of books offering insight on the parenting process. Many of these books have great advice about topics like helping infants sleep through the night, encouraging sharing in preschoolers, or improving homework habits for grade-schoolers. Others focus on a particular area, like discipline or health, or a specific group of kids, such as toddlers or children dealing with particular issues. Rarely is there a book that is as applicable for new parents as for those that have been around the block a few times. I believe *The "Perfect" Parent* is one of those books. It is not just about the parent or just about the child but about building the relationship between them through communication.

I was lucky enough to meet Roma through a mutual friend and was instantly impressed by her passion and compassion. We became partners in founding Tools of Growth, which provides parents with communication tools to raise kids to "Be Happy, Think Positive, and Do Good."

Roma has spent years dedicating herself to understanding both what goes into making a good parent-child relationship and how to share this with others practically. She has a way of distilling information so that it is accessible to all of us. She sees the same parenting behaviors that many of us have witnessed, but she has a way of looking at them differently. I try daily to put Roma's words into practice; I just wish I had had her wisdom to guide me from the beginning!

In the following pages, Roma will show you how you can draw on your inner resources—what she calls your inner perfection—to enhance the way you communicate with your children, building trust, and thereby making it second nature for them to reach out to you, ultimately strengthening your bond with your kids for life. I hope her words are as inspiring to you as they have been for me.

—Julie Watson, PhD

Introduction

Imagine that your young children, facing a long lineup of parents, are told they are free to choose any mother or father from the group. Who do you think they'd pick? I guarantee it would be you and *only you*. Why? Because *you* are the only parent they have ever known. *You* are the one they call "Mom" or "Dad." *You* are the one they love and adore. *You*, alone, understand them like none other. Your presence in their life brings them joy and your absence, incompleteness. You share a deep and complete bond. In their eyes, *you* are the "perfect" parent.

But what does the word "perfect" really mean? According to the Oxford dictionary, the definition of the word is: *having all the required or desirable elements, qualities, or characteristics.* Now, like me, you might not think you're anywhere near perfect. But when it comes to your children, you already have all that they require and desire. You might be a parent who is emotionally charged, one who is calm and collected, or somewhere in between. It's irrelevant to them. To your kids, you are perfect, just the way you are.

The irony is that we spend huge amounts of time and energy giving in to the pressure of highest expectations, pursuing some idealized version of perfection, when, in fact, it's already within us. Yes, we are our own children's "perfect" parents, and within us lie all the simple, yet profound qualities of inner perfection. When we embrace this perfection, we come not only to intellectually *understand* but also to *feel* that we are fully equipped for our grand role of parenting.

This is when we truly comprehend that within us we have what *we* need to fulfill all that *they* need—which is simply for them to live a happy life.

I first began to understand this myself shortly after my daughter, Nitasha, was born. The year was 1988. Nitasha was six months old, and I had settled pretty well into parenting by then. My dad and I were in the family room, and it was naptime for the baby. I put her down in her playpen with a bottle while we sat close by, watching her chug her milk and struggle to keep her eyes open.

"She's beautiful," said the proud grandfather. "Can you imagine your life without her now?"

"I can't. I just can't," I responded as I watched her doze off. When I turned to look at my father again, my mind jumped back four years. "How did you ever send me off, all the way to the U.S., Papa?" I asked. "Weren't you worried sick when I moved here?"

I had been born and raised in Kuwait, and I left that country and my parents at age twenty, to marry my husband and live in Los Angeles.

"A little bit," my dad nodded, Indian style. "But seeing you happy pacified all our fears. All your mom and I wanted for you was to see you happy and to do what's right for you. It's the same thing you'd want for your Nitasha."

His words made me think. Really, was that true? Was that all I wanted for her? I hadn't really thought about it . . . not yet, at least. Like all new parents, I had been busy—giving birth, getting used to sleepless nights, nursing, learning to function on so little rest. But now I wondered: Was happiness *all* I really wanted for Nitasha?

"Actually, Papa," I answered after a moment of reflection, "I want her to be happy, and I also want her to do well for herself, to be kind and smart, to have good morals, to make lots of friends . . ." My list went on and on.

"That's all great," he said, this time with both the typical Indian nod and hand wave, "but you'd want her to be happy first, no? And that builds the foundation for all the rest. When she's happy, she'll be more prepared to do what's right for her—or as you said, to 'do well for herself.'"

He was right. He *is* right. If a child is happy to begin with, then all the other accomplishments naturally follow.

"What exactly do we want for our children?" is a question that I have answered many more times since that day. I have answered it for myself, and I have heard it answered by others. Now I ask that same question at the beginning of all my parenting classes. And the first response that every parent gives is, "I want my child to be happy!" After that, the other things parents desire can be summed up by saying they want their child to think positive and to do good, for themselves and those around them.

This is what my grandparents wanted for my parents, what my parents wanted and still want for me. It's what I want for my children—Nitasha and her younger brother, Navin—and it's also undoubtedly what you want for yours.

There is another important question, though, that we rarely ask ourselves: *What are we seeking for ourselves from parenting?* Have we ever wondered about the long-term goal of parenting or even asked ourselves, *What do I want from this parenting ride? What's in it for me?*

Only after my kids left for college could I look back and understand that what I wanted for myself had little to do with well-behaved and high-achieving children. In the short term, of course, as we all do, I wanted good kids who would respect me, listen to me, love me, and so on. But once I was no longer immersed in their day-to-day routines, I realized that what I had worked for all along was not just "good children" but a "good relationship" with my children. What a revelation!

In fact, what we hope to achieve in our role as parents is not unlike what we want from marriage, which is encapsulated in the traditional wedding vows: *to have and to hold, for better or for worse, for richer or poorer, in sickness and in health, to love and to cherish until death do us part.* Our goal in marriage is to choose a partner with whom we can share this kind of great, mutually fulfilling relationship—someone who will endure the ups and downs of life with us, who will weather the challenges and the curveballs. That is what we are looking for when we make a lifelong commitment. Parenting is another such formative life commitment with the same goal, don't you think? Isn't it our aim to nurture a healthy relationship that withstands difficulties and that flourishes and grows stronger with the passage of time, alongside the obvious day-to-day challenges?

This is exactly why, I came to realize, I got great satisfaction from the fact that as my kids grew up and went off to college, made independent choices, and were no longer under our roof, they would still turn to me for counsel or advice or just to meet for lunch or coffee. Their desire to spend time with us was proof that they valued and respected what we had built together: a good relationship. It became clear to me that despite all the highs and lows of their growing-up years—the struggles, the grapples, the tears, and the fears—having a strong relationship with us was equally important to our kids and their happiness.

A few years later, I would read surveys and research that supported my conclusion. In fact, young people said that spending time with family and their connection with parents was what made them happy, first and foremost.[1] It turns out that having a good relationship is fulfilling not just for us, the parents, but for our children as well.

As we all know, communication is the key to a healthy relationship. Without it, we feel shut out, unloved, stuck, at a dead end. The strength of any relationship is built step by step, not with a single exchange but through the process of day-to-day talking, listening, and resolving differences. *Communication* is not just about being able to express our feelings; it's about tailoring our words so we can get through to our kids and come to common ground. Think about the root of that word: It has to do with "communing," with coming together. When we truly communicate, we connect— we build a good relationship. And who better to do this with than our own children.

Ultimately, it is this effort, this intention to create a connection that brings us true *joy*, which is more than simply a feeling or an emotion— it's a state of fulfilling happiness. Indeed, my ongoing relationship with my children has filled me with joy, and so will yours.

My observations about the relationships between parents and children have been influenced tremendously by those who write about personal growth, or as I like to call it, personal empowerment. By the time my son, Navin, went off to college, I had already spent a good seven years passionately exploring this field. The knowledge and understanding I gained from reading works by Deepak Chopra, Louise Hay, Wayne Dyer, and others had started to flow into my core parenting habits. As these writers prompted me to think about my inner landscape—my thoughts and feelings, that is—I began to grasp the infinite potential of my own parental instincts. Understanding myself took the edge off parenting. The whole experience became smoother: I started to *respond* calmly instead of just reacting emotionally. I became more observant. I found myself laughing louder, loving more deeply, learning from my kids, and managing emotions better—both mine and theirs. I became a more confident parent.

Something similar was happening with my children. They were now moving successfully into the next phase of their life, displaying more responsibility and greater independence. This is not to say, by any means, that this was the end of our parenting challenges. There were many more to come, and there still are. However, I felt equipped to manage any difficulties, as did the kids. By now, they had a solid foundation. They had figured out how to face their problems; they understood that mistakes were to be learned from. They could lift themselves up from falls, and best of all, they trusted that we were there for them, for their guidance—and they took us up on that, whenever necessary.

This didn't go unnoticed by friends and family, who approached me with questions about how I handled parenting victories and what sometimes seem like parenting failures. I was delighted to share what I had learned with as many parents as I could, at every opportunity.

Deepak Chopra says that "coincidences are not accidents but signals from the universe, which can guide us toward our true destiny."[2] It was destiny, then, that through a common friend I met Julie Watson, who has a PhD in developmental psychology and is a research consultant for children's media and technology. Julie would become not just a friend but also my future business partner, and she soon introduced me to the concept of emotional intelligence (EI).

As I jumped into the works of the pioneers in that field, Dr. Daniel Goleman and Dr. John Gottman, I was awed to see all the research that had been done on EI and its role in parenting effectively, along with its life-altering benefits to children. I always knew emotional management (as I thought of it) to be an important part of personal empowerment. But I had not realized there were so many scientific findings on the benefits of emotional intelligence specifically for children and parents. In 2007, very little of this information had made it into the mainstream. As I immersed myself in the research—reading, attending classes, joining online forums, and so forth—I found myself fusing emotional intelligence with what I had learned from the thought leaders about personal empowerment. It was the perfect fit—personal empowerment in parenting, supported with cutting-edge science.

With this fresh perspective, I had even more success helping friends who approached me expressing all-too-common parental concerns:

I'm pregnant, and I'm nervous about the future.

I have teenage kids, and I'm tired of the arguing.

I'm afraid I'm not spending enough time with my preschooler.

My six-year-old daughter defies me about everything. What am I doing wrong?

How can I make sure my son does his homework? I feel like I'm making things worse by nagging.

My child doesn't listen to me.

Even though I try my best, I feel so guilty. Am I a bad parent?

I was getting calls with questions like these from a dozen friends, several times a week each, and spending a lot of time talking them through approaches and solutions, when one of them proposed something I hadn't thought of: Would I teach a class on parenting to a small group of women?

"But I have no credentials," I said, puzzled.

Her answer was direct: "Your practical approach to parenting . . . your relationship with your kids—those are your credentials." She pointed out that every piece of advice I had given her—and all of the other parents—had been easy and had worked for their kids and made them feel more comfortable and confident as parents.

The half dozen moms and I met over the next few months, and as word spread, I followed up with another group of friends, and then another. I began to think that the answers to their questions and this whole approach to raising kids to be happy, make good choices, and rise to their potential—what I've come to characterize as Tools of Growth—should be shared with a broader audience.

And that has led to this book.

There are topics you won't find here, like how to potty train your child or how to pick the right elementary school or even how to discipline your children. This is not a parenting handbook that covers the specifics of every developmental stage of childhood.

What you can expect here is a short, sweet, easy-to-grasp guide to changing your perspective on parenting, simplifying the ride, and amplifying the enjoyment. Best of all, you can expect a surefire path to building not just a good, but a *great* lasting and long-term relationship with your kids. This is a guide that helps lighten up the all too familiar parental quandaries of *This is so hard—I don't know if I can do this!* The *What if I mess up my child?* and *Will my child turn out okay?* In other words, it's a guide that helps pacify the doubt, guilt, fear, and worry all parents feel about their own potential and the future of their kids. It is a simple yet profound guide that will help you recognize and tap into your inner perfection. It will build your parental confidence, which will be reflected in the self-confidence of your children. How? Through five simple, effective, science-supported communication tools that help you use your inner perfection to connect with your kids.

This book will help you uncover hidden resources within yourself that will guide you to communicate more effectively with your kids. Put simply, it will help you relax into the long-term role of parenting. It is a roadmap that reassures you that you are, indeed, the "perfect" parent.

So whether you are a parent-to-be, a new parent, or a seasoned one, by the end of this book you'll see how your own personal growth can flow into the personal growth of your kids and your entire family. As you empower yourself, you will empower and equip not just your kids but also your entire network of family and friends. Through scientific evidence, it will become clear why and how understanding and managing your own emotions will help you understand and manage your children's.

After you've understood each of the five communication tools and begun practicing them, do keep the book nearby and consult it whenever you're facing a parenting obstacle. At the end of each chapter you will find affirmation reminders and quick takeaways recapping the points that have been made. And at the back of this book you'll also find the "Perfect" Parent Toolbox, a useful, grab-and-go, at-a-glance reference that recaps the chapter-ending affirmation reminders and takeaways and that can serve as a great refresher as you work through day-to-day issues. Before you know it, you will be turning your communication breakdowns into communication breakthroughs, and you will start to enjoy the wild ride of parenting consistently and deeply.

The end result? You will raise your kids to be happy, think positive, and do good in their lives, despite any challenges. And you'll earn the priceless gift of a great long-term relationship with your kids.

In joy!

Get Ready for a Parenting Makeover

When you change the way you look at things,
the things that you look at change.

—*Dr. Wayne Dyer*

How many times this week did you recite the "gotta" mantra?

Before you're even fully awake, you're thinking, *I gotta get them up. I gotta get their breakfast and lunches ready. I gotta make sure they have their homework in their backpacks.* As you start to relax into your two-minute power-shower, you're rudely interrupted with *Oh, yes, I gotta make sure to pick them up on time* and *I gotta get them to soccer practice on time, this time.* Then there's *Oh, no, I'm snack parent this week, so I gotta pick up granola bars and Gatorade for the team after practice today—gotta do that as soon as I drop them off . . . Gotta! Gotta! Gotta!*

As parents, we find it all too easy to get stuck in a day-to-day rut of frantic multitasking. After all, multitasking is a necessary skill today, not only to keep up with a parent's busy schedule but also to manage a child's activities. It's true in all stages and phases of parenthood.

When we are pregnant, we are thinking about the arrival of the baby. When the baby arrives, we are worrying over feedings and sleep times. As our children get more mobile, we start to safety-proof the house. As they start talking, we are making sure they have LeapFrog and phonics builders to facilitate learning to read. Then we are scheduling kindergarten, dance classes, and sports and preparing them for elementary school and beyond. Before we know it, we are planning their departure into the wider world.

Where does the time go? If you're already asking yourself this perennial question, you aren't alone. More often than they care to admit, some parents even seem eager to step off this crazy carousel called *parenthood*. "I can't wait until he turns eighteen and moves out! I'm so done," said one mom, a financial analyst.

Six months later she was singing a different tune: "I can't believe he doesn't even call home anymore. Let's cut off his allowance, and then we'll see how he survives."

A year later, it was, "He has a job now and a girlfriend. He doesn't really need me anymore. What a selfish, spoiled brat!" She gasped. "I spent twenty years of my life on him. Not one or two or five or seven. *Twenty!* Where did it go? Where's the return on investment? I invested twenty years in parenthood—day in, day out. And now he says he wants to live his own life! What happened? What did I do wrong?"

For her, as for most parents, it's just that life happened. We get so busy with the daunting *do's* of our tasks that we forget to *be*. We get so caught up in multitasking—hyper-tasking, actually—and planning ahead that we take the fun out of our parental ride. The kids don't do that to us; we do it to ourselves. They don't arrive with an agenda; we put them (and ourselves) on one. And then before you know it, busy-ness becomes a habit. We get so busy being busy that we forget to connect. Just as I did.

One summer, late on a hot Saturday afternoon, my husband, Harry, and I returned with the kids after back-to-back games—soccer for my daughter, basketball for my son—and a trip to the craft store to pick up supplies for a school project. Ten minutes after we walked in the door, I barely had a chance to change clothes and visit the bathroom, and I was already thinking ahead. I walked up to the kids, who had plopped themselves in front of the TV with their dad. I heard myself saying, "Okay, you have thirty minutes to watch TV. Then, Nitasha, you need to start working on your project. And Navin, you need to clean up your room and take a shower. By six thirty we have to start getting ready for your cousin's birthday party."

The response was immediate. "Oh, no, Mom, I'm tired," complained Nitasha. "I don't want to work on the project today. We have all day Sunday."

My son chimed in. "Can I clean my room tomorrow, Mom? Pleeeease?" he begged. "I'm still sweating and hot."

"We have to go to temple tomorrow," I countered. "Then we'll take the rest of Sunday off." I laid out my rationale. "We have to go with the plan. If we have a productive weekend, you'll be ready for the week."

My husband let me finish, then he pulled me into the other room and said, "What is this, boot camp? We left the house at nine in the morning and got home at three thirty. You're giving them just a half-hour break and then it's off to more stuff? Come on, they're kids!"

"But you don't understand," I went on, defending myself. "There's a project that needs to be started, and if we don't get started, nothing will get done."

"I get it," he said. "Yes, it needs to be done. But it does not *all* need to be talked about *right now*. The kids have had a busy day. It was hot as heck outside. We just got home, and less than fifteen minutes later, you're planning the rest of their weekend. I'm glad I'm not them!"

We argued for a few minutes more, and as I stomped away, I heard my husband say, "You know they're not going to remember what you did for them. They're going to remember the times you spent with them doing nothing."

"Right!" I barked back. "And while I do nothing, I'm sure you'll help them with their projects and homework during the week, as you always do," I added sarcastically.

I went up to my bedroom, furious with my husband's lack of appreciation for all the planning that I put into managing our kids. I turned the TV on and plopped down on my chaise, still fuming. I was flipping channels when, as fate would have it, I tuned in to hear Oprah, who, as we all know, has a knack for being at the right place at the right time. Her guest was Dr. Alvin Rosenfeld, who was discussing "what kids really need" and introducing his book *The Over-Scheduled Child: Avoiding the Hyper-Parenting Trap*.

Dr. Rosenfeld—a graduate of Cornell University and Harvard Medical School, and a board-certified child, adolescent, and adult psychiatrist on the faculty of Stanford University's medical school— was explaining his groundbreaking research on "why it is better—in the short and long run—for parents and kids alike to slow down, do less, and generally turn the volume down on family life."[3] He assured viewers that the message in his book would make parents feel happier and calmer about their children and help them raise children who succeed in life.

His message struck a nerve. We all *want* to be ideal parents, but we seem to be too busy raising our kids to stop and nurture them. We fool ourselves into thinking it is more important to provide things for them than it is to be with them. We might be around them a lot, doing things for them, but we are not necessarily dialed in. So *that's* what we do wrong: We disconnect.

Perhaps you are driving your kids to school, and one child starts to tell a funny story about a friend, but you're not listening. You've tuned out. Instead of listening to and enjoying what your child is saying, you're planning what you are going to do after you've dropped him off. All of a sudden, when your other child starts laughing, you jump back in, pretending to know what was said and joining in the laughter. You may feel bad, but you're not alone. We've all experienced disconnected moments like this.

"How can I stay connected when I'm so busy?" asked a young mom in one of my parenting classes. "Doesn't doing things for my kids mean we are connected? This is so hard."

Another mom admitted:

> My life was hectic. I got sick of feeling guilty all the time for the way I responded to my kids. I figured that is just the way I am. I was too busy to deal with feelings—theirs or my own—so I buried the emotions somewhere and moved from task to task, from one day to the next. Then one lucky day, as I got done screaming at my nine-year-old son for not starting his homework when we had to leave for basketball practice in an hour, I overheard my twelve-year-old daughter tell a friend over the

phone, "Yeah, that's just my mom. She can be a b%^#* sometimes . . . actually, most of the time."

All those feelings this mother had buried away came out and created havoc. "I was devastated," she remembered. "I just burst out crying. I must have cried for a half hour straight. I would never have talked about my own mom like that. Besides, if this is what my daughter thinks of me now, heading into the teen years when she most needs guidance, she'll never trust me or turn to me later. Am I just a bad parent?"

If you hear inner voices too often saying, *What did I do wrong? This is so hard! Am I a bad parent?*—it's a sign that you have lost touch somewhere. Repetitive questions of doubt and guilt signal us to get off the multitasking highway and slow down. Somewhere along the line it has become more important to *do* stuff than to *feel* stuff. Dance practice (or whatever is on the day's agenda) has become no longer an opportunity to watch our kids and spend time with them, but merely an activity we drop them off at while we multitask with other errands. At one point or another, we've all done that.

What's interesting is that we all start out with the right idea in mind: *Let's start a family. Let's multiply our love. Let's make a little you-and-me. Let's bring a miracle into this world. This will be the happiest moment of our lives.* But somehow, along the way, those original thoughts got lost in the hustle and bustle of life.

Don't get me wrong. We don't love our kids any less because we're busy. They are always the focal point. They are at the center of our attention and our universe. They are our very heartbeat, and we would do anything for them. But as we drop them off at dance practice, do we ever think about our larger goal: our relationship with our kids? Do we consider what would happen if we spent an hour, even once a week, watching them practice and cheering them on? Do we recognize that it would make us feel more connected and that the kids would love for us to be their audience? Think about it: When the kids have performances, they are not looking for the faces of their friends' parents in the audience. They are looking for our faces, our smiles, our applause. So why wait for a performance to share the good feeling? Why not sprinkle a little bit of it in the day-to-day? That, exactly, would be working toward that deeper connection and relationship with our kids.

All the time, it seems, our minds are running fast and our bodies are racing to keep up. We are bypassing how we feel emotionally and perhaps even physically in order to get it all done. It's time to stop for a reality check: Remember, our kids are on this ride with us. Ask most parents as they drop off their children at that dance lesson, "Who are you doing this for?" The answer invariably will be, "I am doing this for my kids!" We are cramming our kids' agendas so they can be or have this or that—so when they grow up, they will remember they were loved and well provided for.

Well, the truth is that kids will remember less what we did for them and more how we spoke and reacted to them. And, as my husband reminded me that hot Saturday afternoon, they will remember the quality time we spent with them more than the hours we spent rushing them from place to place. If we are constantly on the go, we'll have less energy and patience in dealing with them. This means we will have less presence of mind to help them manage their emotions when they're up against a challenge, let alone manage our own.

In other words, if you're using most of your energy to *do stuff* for your kids, then you'll have that much less energy to just *be there* for them. Yes, stuff needs to get done—there's no doubt about that. Assignments must be finished, and hungry children are by no means agreeable children. But if our focus stays only on the things that need to done, we put ourselves in a lose-lose position in the long run. Both parent and child lose out on experiencing the full potential of shared moments and a magnificent relationship. We get caught up in the schedules, the arguments, the screaming, and the yelling, and we end up feeling guilty, doubting ourselves, and worrying about our children. We have defeated the purpose of why we became parents in the first place.

Guilt, doubts, and fears are walls that we inadvertently put up in front of that doorway to a positive relationship, and the longer we leave those walls up, the more we bump into them. As busy-ness sets in and life takes over, we even forget what was behind those walls— the desire for a healthy relationship with our kids. To get back to the basics, we need to knock down the walls and remember what we wanted before they went up. By simply taking a few moments out of your busy day to connect with your child and yourself, you will see those walls starting to crumble. Rays of light will peek through, reminding you of what you had in mind when you first committed to having your children: *Let's multiply our love.*

Tuning In

Reworking your life in order to be and to feel, along with all the other "to do's" on your list, might seem daunting. But let me assure you, it's simply a shift in perspective. If you're still reading this book and can relate to the stories, then you're beginning to think, *Hmm, yup, that's me . . . and that's me.* It's all sounding familiar, and if I'm right, then you are already looking at things differently. You've already started to make a change in your thinking. So . . . welcome to parenthood all over again! You are starting to tune in and connect with yourself.

How will this help? First, it will empower you to look at your core parenting habits from the outside. You will be able to take a step back and, as with a video recording, play back and review the events and issues of the day. Then, with a little more practice, you will be able to consider issues and events live, as they are happening. You'll become aware of how your kids react to your cues and how you respond, and vice versa. Tuning in makes you a more conscious parent, one who is ready to grow and expand his or her parenting experience.

If you can imagine these steps, you are on your way to a parenting makeover. If you're having trouble, take a breath, reread these paragraphs, and visualize the words as you read them. Just observe how you feel inside. Your slowing breath and heart rate and the good energy you are feeling right now are signaling that you are tuned in. And that's really all you need to get started: to feel that you are tuned in, that you are present at the first step toward growth.

A Parenting Makeover

For starters, ***memorize the goal***—a great relationship with your kids. How do you get there? With good communication. Repeat this to yourself as often as you can: *Good communication is the way to a great relationship with my kids.* When you keep your eye on your goal, you position yourself to achieve that goal. If you need a visual reminder, post this guiding statement or affirmation on your refrigerator, put it on your to-do bulletin board, or enter it in your phone as a note.

Writing goals down and keeping them in plain view is a great way to remind ourselves of our underlying intention, especially on busy days (which, for most parents, is almost every day). The more often we revisit goals or look at them in written form, the more we start to feel, think, and act on them, aligning them, naturally, with our intentions. Before we know it, our goals will become part of who we are and what we do. They will start to flow effortlessly into our daily parenting habits.

Focusing on your parenting goal is how you will start to change the way you look at things. And when you make a habit of keeping good communication in mind as a way to achieve that goal, I promise you, the things that challenge you now as a parent will start to shift in your favor. Your internal shift in perspective will lead to a noticeable shift for the better in the recurring family situations that presented a challenge before. The return on investment is that great relationship with your kids. But don't be surprised if, as a bonus, you introduce your inner self to your outer self—and your current self to a new you.

Next, *align your actions with your goal* of achieving a great relationship through good communication. More often than not, we set out to do a certain thing but end up going in a completely different direction. For example, every parent's inner desire is to raise children to be independent. Yet all day long, we tell our kids what to do, making them more and more dependent on us. Perhaps your aim is to help your son with homework—biology was always a challenge for mine—but every day you end up bickering about it, as I did. It was a daily tug of war: I wanted Navin to spend extra time focusing on what was his most difficult subject, and he would end up pushing it off, loitering around, and finding a way to avoid it. Getting him started was an ordeal every single time.

One day I was so frustrated that I asked myself, "Why can't I do this constructively? Why does he fight me on this? Why is this such a struggle, when all I really want to do is help?" Once again, the big question was, "What am I doing wrong?" The answer was staring me in the face: My purpose was to get Navin to be responsible for his biology homework, but the actions I was taking were not at all aligned with that goal. It was a communication meltdown at its best.

Only when I finally opened up a dialogue with him about the issue were we able to constructively resolve it together. Communication helped us minimize and then successfully undo the repeated struggle.

Parental communication is effective when what we want on the inside—that big-picture goal of relationship-building—actually aligns with what happens on the outside—the actions. In other words, we communicate effectively when how we behave in a situation with our kids matches up with our goal of having a good relationship with them! Otherwise we face a tornado of unwanted and confusing emotions. When recurring issues go unaddressed, frustrations, doubts, fears, and guilt about parenting set in, snowballing from one issue to another, from one encounter to the next, hurting the parent, the child, and the relationship.

When you experience a communication breakdown, you will notice that you did not accomplish what you set out to do. Somehow, somewhere, you disconnected. With school-age children, this may happen a few times a month; as kids get older, into their adolescent years, it could be a few times a week or maybe even several times each day. Unfortunately, the meltdowns eventually become our standard communication habit, and this is what drains the fun out of parenting and invites negative emotions in where they don't belong—into our home and into our family.

But fear not! The five tools shared in this book will show you how you can reverse this process. Whether you are having a few issues a day or a few ongoing challenges a week, whether you are a new parent or a seasoned one, there is always room for growth. It's time to stop the cycle of repeated communication breakdowns and start fresh. It's time for a makeover. It's time to step back, refuel, refresh your parenting experience, and start seeing results. It's time to align your actions with your goal. And the way to do that is through effective communication. It's time to let our intentions speak for themselves.

And if you are a parent-to-be, then you are way ahead of the game. You have nothing to undo. These tools are a great opportunity for you to get a head start on developing effective communication from the beginning. Practice them to enhance communication with your spouse, friends, or family.

Our Parental Guidance System

Now that we know that effective communication (or the lack of it) can make or break us as parents, let's get familiar with our Parental Guidance System, or PGS. Much like the GPS of a car, our PGS can assist communication by helping us navigate through the mysterious unknowns on the long road of parental life.

Our PGS is made up of two important components—parental instinct and communications tools—and we need to identify and comprehend both in order to align *what we want* (our larger goal of a great relationship) with our actions (*how we communicate* with our children).

Our Parental Instinct

The primary component of our PGS is our parental instinct—the natural intuitive power that all parents have in common.

Perhaps you feel confident in your instinctive sense as a parent, or maybe, like me, you first questioned whether that intuition is an inherent part of you or a learned skill. When I gave birth to my daughter, I remember waking up in the hospital to find my mother holding and rocking my new baby. I was twenty-three. Startled, I asked my mother, "When did you get here?"

"About a half hour ago," she replied. "The baby was crying, so I thought I'd hold her."

"I didn't even know you were here," I said, suddenly in a panic. "Mom, what if I do this when I take the baby home? What if I don't hear her cry at night?"

Like most new parents, I had all kinds of self-doubt. In her thoroughly Indian accent, and with a big, indulgent laugh, my mother replied, "Oh no, you won't, *beta* [my child]. When you become a parent, a natural instinct comes alive inside of you, and that will wake you up every time. I promise you. Just wait and see."

She was right. When our children come into our lives, something does "come alive" inside us. This new love heightens our natural instincts for protecting and taking care of our children. This parental instinct is not something we consciously choose but simply a gift of parenting. And it is not given only to those who give birth. It is within anyone who assumes the responsibility of being a parent.

I was reminded of this again when my daughter was two and a half. Nitasha had been fussy all day, and in the early hours of the next morning, she had woken up and was whimpering softly. Though the baby monitor was not on, I somehow felt something was wrong and woke up instinctively to check on her. Tiptoeing into the room, I touched her forehead. Sure enough, she had a high fever. I gave her some Tylenol, rocked her for a bit, and then brought her to our bed. Instantly, my sound-asleep husband woke up, and there he was, helping me figure out what to do.

At the time, I was six months pregnant with my son, Navin, and my husband suggested that I go back to sleep while he took charge and kept an eye on the baby. I remember wondering later that day how this man—who is not a morning person, who usually takes a half hour just to get out of bed, and who is not fully awake until his first cup of tea—was so wide-eyed and ready to tackle the day at four thirty in the morning. He, too, was equipped with this intuitive power, this instinct—just as every parent is.

Whether or not we recognize it right away, our parental instinct dictates our priorities, regardless of our agenda for the day. You could be in the middle of an important meeting at work, and if the school calls and says your child has taken a fall, you will drop everything to be there. A sick child has the power of rearranging our to-do list for the day, the week, or as long as the child needs us. Whether you are the president of the United States or a working mom like me, your parental instinct tells you to put your kids first. It pushes you to protect and connect with your kids above all else.

Why is it, then, that this purest of instincts is mostly expressed and understood when something has gone wrong? We instinctively rush to the aid of our children when they are hurt or unwell, and our children know securely that we are there for them. They know that we understand their pain and will do all we can to ease them through it. And yet, on an ordinary day, the same children might say, "You just don't get it," or "Leave me alone," or "Why can't you be nice, Mom?" Or the worst: "I hate you!" They know, feel, and see our love during some problem but not in the day-to-day. If our kids actually felt that all our efforts were geared toward helping them—not just in a crisis, but every single moment—then we'd never, ever hear heartbreaking comments like those.

For a moment, imagine that your children truly understood that you are always looking out for them. Imagine your twelve-year-old son saying, "You're right, Mom, I need to get started with my biology homework. Even if I don't like that subject, I understand that the work needs to be done to pass the class. Can you please help me with it?" Wouldn't that be amazing?

How do we accomplish this? How can we have them not just know but truly *believe* that we *always* have their best interest at heart? Through the five tools of effective communication that we are about to explore!

This is not to say that they will *always* remember that we have their best interest in mind. But I can assure you that any "I hate you" comments will be less frequent. And if they do occur, your kids will feel bad and apologize afterward—because they know and trust that you are there for them and have their best interest at heart; they know that they can communicate with you openly and comfortably.

Communication—coming together—can only be successful if we are able to get our point across to our kids. Communication is ineffective when we are simply seeking our own interests or venting our own frustrations. But communication *is* effective when we create a common neutral ground or space where our children are comfortable expressing their thoughts and feelings while we are listening. Communication is at its best when they feel they are and will be heard. To accomplish that, we could all use some help—some tools—which takes us to the second component of our Parental Guidance System.

The Five Communication Tools

The purpose of these communication tools is to fuse your parental instinct with your day-to-day communication habits. These tools will make it possible, even simple, to align what you as a parent actually want—your goal of a great relationship with your kids—with how you communicate that to your children every day. Of course, life is not consistent, and at times you or your child will slip up and have an occasional outburst. But how incredible would it be, when there's a flare-up of tempers at home, if everyone had the tools to understand the issue, fix the problem, make peace, and learn from the experience?

Those tools are within reach. All it takes to use them is some practice.

These five communication tools are essential for effective parenting and will help you raise kids who are happy, who think positive, and who do good. With repetition, they will become communication *habits* that are guaranteed to benefit you, your kids, and your whole parenting experience, both now and in years to come. These are the tools that will lead you to your goal of achieving a great relationship with your kids.

So what are these all-important tools? We can see them revealed in the words that we will use to define happy, relaxed, and effective parenting: honorable, approachable, sensible, reasonable and responsible, enjoyable and memorable. As Aldous Huxley said in *Brave New World*, "Words can be like X-rays, if you use them properly—they'll go through anything. You read and you're pierced." These particular words will help you shift your perspective in a sweet parenting makeover!

And as we delve into each of these five communication tools, we will also explore the research behind them so you can tune in to both the art and the science of effective parenting.

Beginning with *Honorable Parenting,* we will uncover and strengthen the inner core of communication, thereby planting confidence both *in* and *between* you and your child. *Approachable Parenting* will assist you in building a two-way trust that will last a lifetime. With *Sensible Parenting* we will explore using each one of your five senses to nurture connections with your children. *Reasonable and Responsible Parenting* will help you branch out further through mutual understanding. Finally, we will reveal the secrets behind *Enjoyable and Memorable*

Parenting—the background musical notes that allow you to savor the fruits of your best efforts at parenting.

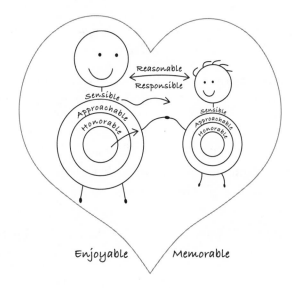

Introducing you to these tools is my first intention with this book. For them to be most effective, however, you'll have to promise to embrace them, use them regularly, and make them your own. You'll have to turn them into lifelong family communication habits and make them second nature. And my second intention with this book is to make these communication habits easy enough to absorb, recall, and apply through simple understanding. Before you know it, you will see how these five communication tools drive your parental instincts to the door of your larger goal—a good relationship with your kids. When that happens, here's what will follow:

- You will be fully equipped to align your actions
  with your goal.

- You will not end up being frustrated, doubtful, guilty, or angry with your children as often as you are now.

- You will not end up blaming yourself for reacting to your children the way you did because you were tired, overwhelmed, or upset about something totally unrelated.

- You will not blame your children for being irrational, being overly emotional, defying limits, or pushing buttons intentionally.

- And when outbursts occur, you'll be able to put them in perspective, regain respect, come together with your kids on the issues, move on, and bounce back constructively.

As you read on, you will notice that these five communication tools emerge from your very own personality—your own inner perfection.

We all know that parenthood is the most ever-changing and ever-challenging ride of our life. This ride, which is supposed to be the "time of our life," may get a little bumpy along the way. With your PGS—your parental instinct and your communication tools—fully equipped, however, you will lift your parenting experience substantially and visibly. You will enhance your confidence, your effectiveness, and ultimately your relationship with your kids, all the while building *their* courage and ability to resolve issues, boosting their self-esteem and self-worth. By the end of this book, you will have a keen, fresh perspective on parenting. You will not just believe but even say out loud: *I use my inner perfection to connect with my kids! I am the "perfect" parent for my child!*

Get ready to start enjoying the ride!

Affirmation Reminder

Each day, through good communication, I am building a great relationship with my child.

 Quick Takeaways

- By shifting your perspective you can give yourself a parenting makeover.

- Tuning in requires memorizing your goal—a great relationship with your kids—and knowing that it is important to align your actions with that goal.

- Effective communication is the bridge that aligns our actions with our parenting goal.

- Use your Parental Guidance System (PGS)—your innate parental instinct and your communication tools.

Honorable Parenting:
Planting Self-Confidence

Confidence . . . thrives on honesty, honor, on the
sacredness of obligations, on faithful protection and on
unselfish performance. Without them it cannot live.

—*Franklin D. Roosevelt*

"What a miracle!" These were the first words that came to my mind
each time my miracles were born, at 7:36 a.m. on May 3, 1988, and
at 7:17 a.m. on January 10, 1991. In fact, the words were not exactly
thoughts but feelings that overflowed from my heart. I didn't really
know what a miracle felt like before I had my kids.

In the United States alone, almost 11,000 miracles are born every
day. And every day this miraculous feeling is experienced and these
words are repeated some 11,000 times. I've felt it and said it, and so

have you. Even if you are not a parent yet but are soon to be one, you already know that a miracle is on its way to you.

And the best part is that our miracles, our gifts from life, are not momentary or temporary—they're here to stay. They are gifts that we receive but also our gifts to *give to*—to love, to cuddle, to take care of, to nurture for years and years to come. From the moment they arrive, their very presence keeps us flowing. We know from the onset that we will spend a lifetime paying our love forward. We will guide these miracles, groom them, and help them grow. We are their first teachers. We will teach them to take their first steps. We will teach them their first words, including the magic words, *please* and *thank you*. We will teach them to get along with others. We will teach them to ride a bike for the very first time, and we will nurse their boo-boos when they fall. Most important, we will teach them resilience. We will teach them how to get up and go at it again.

We are not only their teachers; we are also their biggest fans, their protectors, and their guardians. I find it amazing that all the different roles we play in their lives are packed into one powerful word: *parent*. What's more amazing is that we assume this awesome responsibility willingly, even eagerly.

And yet too often we go through our family lives without giving this role much thought. This is not to say that we are not good role models for our kids but that we don't stop to give ourselves credit for this important commitment.

Let's face it: None of us knew what this ride would be like. We didn't know if we would have healthy children or not; moms didn't know how they would survive the birthing process; and dads didn't know if they had it in them to change a diaper or wake up and comfort a crying little one in the middle of the night. We simply stepped up and hoped for the best.

All along we had, and we continue to have, faith and trust in ourselves. We know we might not always succeed in every decision; we most definitely know that we will stumble many times along the way. But we always have some degree of confidence in ourselves, some conviction that we will get right back up and march forward. We never know what lies ahead, but somehow we have faith that we will make it through. If we didn't, we would not be able to commit to parenthood.

Parenthood is not just a conscious decision. It is also a subconscious commitment to protect our children in the most unselfish performance of our lives, and that commitment manifests itself as confidence. This confidence shines brightest when you—the parent—recognize and honor yourself.

Honoring Yourself

We get no awards for parenthood, even when we do it well. It's not something we get paid for. It is a voluntary position, and volunteering for a lifetime of anything deserves a standing ovation. But to volunteer for a lifetime of responsibility for raising another human being . . . Now that is worth honoring again and again and again. The only one who understands the depth of that kind of dedication is a parent—you.

You are dedicated to guiding your children and shaping them to be responsible adults as best as you can. But remember, while you are helping them grow their own wings, you, too, are growing as a person and a parent every day. You are devoted to this cause because you love your children.

Vedanta, the philosophical portion of the Hindu scriptures, says that love and devotion are the same in their nature but differ only in direction. In other words, I can say I love my kids, but I am devoted to parenting them. I can love them just the way I am, but to parent them means that I have to access my inner self, my higher self. I have to be aware. I have to be awake. I have to be willing to grow with them and for them in order to keep up with them.

I have to be truly present and willing to consciously practice that love with patience. I will be challenged, tested, and tried, I know—probably more times than I ever imagined. And yet I will rise above the challenges and do what is best for my child.

I also know that things will not always go my way. I acknowledge that what is best for my child might not be the best for me; it might not be the way that I wanted or the way that I had envisioned. And yet, if and when needed, I will go beyond my personal likes and dislikes to make things happen for my child. This has to be *devotion*. As often as we can, we want to do our best for our children. As parents, we are all devoted to this purpose, and such devotion is worthy not just of respect but even more so of honor.

When I talk about Honorable Parenting, I like to view the word *honorable* not just as a whole but also as its two components: *honor* and *able*. I like to think about it in the sense of "having the ability to honor" or, in other words, the ability to **accept and respect.**

Honorable Parenting, then, is first and foremost about having the ability to honor yourself for taking on this role. Understand and feel the depth of this devotion, and pat yourself on the back for doing the best that you can, every chance you get. Be your own cheerleader; applaud yourself for attempting to embark on this journey. And for those of you who have already been on this journey for a while, congratulate yourself for the great job that you have done thus far.

"But wait," you might be saying. "I've made so many mistakes!" Of course you have—we all have! That's the only way you can get better at it. Beating yourself up for mistakes you might have made will stall your own growth and, eventually, that of your children. If you commit to learn from your errors, however, you will also teach your kids how to recover, learn, and grow from theirs.

When we accept and respect ourselves and our role as parents, we practice Honorable Parenting. Only when we honor ourselves can we put into perspective the emotions and feelings that are attached to this role.

It's not always easy to do this in our everyday lives, particularly when we're confronted not only with our own personal roadblocks, but with the opinions and perspectives of others, too.

"My husband thinks I sit at home and eat bonbons!" complained one stay-at-home mom. She remarked sadly:

> Little does he know what my day is like! I plan my whole day around the kids' schedules. Even when they are at school, I am busy! Laundry, cleaning, groceries, volunteering at school events, tending to the family needs . . . I am constantly on the go, doing as much as I can. I know I signed up for this, but all it takes is one comment like, "How come you didn't have time to pick up the dry cleaning?" and I'm fuming! I start to feel bad and unappreciated.

Another mom mentioned to her friend, an attorney, that she had needed a break and had left her daughter with her mother and treated herself to a movie matinee. "Must be nice," said the attorney friend in a sarcastic tone of voice.

"I know that I willingly decided to be a stay-at-home mom after we started a family," the mom went on. "And yet I can't help feeling bad or guilty when my working-mom friends make comments like that."

Another mom, a marriage and family therapist who works part time, views the same issue from a different angle. "I don't feel so bad now. I thought only working moms like me felt guilty," she commented as she witnessed this exchange. "I love what I do. It's my passion. And I adore my son—he gives my life purpose. I can't pick one or the other. To feel whole, I have to do both. But to be honest, it's not without a ton of guilt."

Yes, as parents, our journey is filled with emotions like guilt, insecurity, and self-doubt. Often, sometimes unexpectedly, we are bombarded and confused by our own feelings about our decisions. We start to second-guess and doubt ourselves, even though we accept and respect our parenting role in theory. This is hardly unusual; it is parental nature to doubt oneself. Other people's questions about our decisions can hit an open nerve, and other people's comments can play into our emotions and make us feel guilty. So besides accepting and respecting our role as parents, another important part of honoring ourselves is dealing with our emotions; it helps us put issues to rest.

Say a dust storm hits your neighborhood, and you realize a half hour later that you have left a window open. Your first instinct, obviously, is to go and close that window. However, that is not all you do. You can't walk away from the room without cleaning up the dust that has blown in.

Similarly, even when we succeed overall in honoring our role as a parent, emotional storms sometimes leave a bit of a mess. By reminding yourself to honor yourself and your role as a parent, you have merely shut the window and stopped the dust from blowing in. However, the job is not complete until you sweep up the emotional dust that is left behind. It's a two-step process: First, you accept and respect your role. Then you must do what I call "Dealing with the Feeling," which we will discuss shortly. Together, these steps complete the process of becoming an honorable parent—one who has the ability to honor oneself completely, emotions included.

Before we dive into emotional management, we should quickly look at the role that emotions play in balancing communication.

Understanding Your Communication Balance

As we all know, emotions can create havoc with effective communication. If we don't manage our emotions, we allow our emotions to manage us. If we do manage our emotions, however, we can also manage our thoughts, our child's emotions, and, therefore, our response to the situation at hand.

Let's take a minute to understand how thoughts and feelings fit into the landscape of communication. We all have an *inner* communication landscape and an *outer* one, each dedicated to its own purpose. Your inner communication landscape is your internal dialogue—your thoughts and feelings. Your outer communication landscape, on the other hand, is how you express those thoughts and feelings externally, through words, behavior, tone of voice, and body language.

Communication Balance

Thoughts + Feelings (inner communication landscape)

Expressions (outer communication landscape)

Our inner and outer communication landscapes are deeply connected to each other. What we say and how we behave depends on

our feelings and thoughts. If we are not feeling and thinking positively about an issue, chances are it will not be long before those negative thoughts and feelings end up expressing themselves in speech
and actions.

Think of your communication balance as a kind of seesaw.

When your inner communication landscape is balanced, your
outer communication landscape improves as well:

Once you balance your thoughts and feelings, your expressions will follow accordingly, allowing for lasting effective communication. It is these balanced expressions that make an impression on the inner landscape of our children—on their thoughts and feelings. We all know when we are angry and say things harshly, our kids respond harshly—it's a communication breakdown! The negative energy behind our thoughts and feelings emerges in our expressions and reflects directly onto our children. As a result, they fight back and respond negatively too. What we put out is what we get back.

It is our job, as parents, to model effective communication for them. If we are upset about an issue and let our feelings take over before we approach our kids, we make ineffective communication a habit, and what overflows from our anger and harsh words is nothing other than the all too familiar emotions of guilt, doubt, worry, and fear. When these destructive aftermath emotions occur again and again, they hurt the self-esteem, self-worth, and self-confidence of our children as well—taking us far from our goal of building lasting healthy relationships with them.

Similarly, by overthinking things, we can let our intellect outweigh our emotions, with equally poor communication as a result. If we can get into the good habit of balancing our emotions and our thoughts, the result will be balanced expression, which will *always* lead to effective communication.

When my son was in the fourth grade, a friend shared some horror stories about her child's experience with a certain fifth-grade teacher. Naturally, this created an impression in my mind, and alarm bells rang when I found out the following year that my son would be in this teacher's class. Suddenly I was besieged by negative emotions and fears. But there was no other option, because there was no other class available. I did not want to taint my son's thoughts and feelings about this teacher, however. So almost every day I would beat around the bush, trying to gauge his opinion by asking him some indirect question: "How is Miss X?" I would ask. Or, "Is she a good teacher?" "Is she nice?" "Do you understand what she is teaching?"

A month into the school year, my son asked if I had met Miss X yet. "No," I answered.

"So how come you don't like her?" my smarty-pants wondered.

No matter how much we want to conceal our thoughts and feelings, they will always influence our expressions. We can't help it. Our thoughts and feelings are intertwined with our comments and our actions. Together they can help us move forward—or they can push us backward. But if we sort out and lighten the weight of those feelings, we can shift from thinking negatively to thinking positively. This will guide us in responding positively as well, which will bring communication back into balance.

My son had seen right through my doubts and reservations about Miss X. The next day, however, I came up with a great idea: I called a close family friend who also taught at that school and casually asked, "What do you think of Miss X?"

Her response? "She's a great teacher. Very experienced, very patient. Both my kids have been in her class. If Navin has her, he'll do well. It's a good fit."

This was the opposite of what I heard before, and it was information that came from a trusted source—information that could have saved me a great deal of worrying. Why hadn't I thought to call that friend earlier? Because I was too wrapped up in my emotions to think clearly! So then, what made me call her now?

I had turned to that wonderfully effective tool: Dealing with the Feeling.

In his research on emotional intelligence, Dr. Daniel Goleman has written that the emotional brain responds to an event more quickly than our thinking brain. It is obvious, then, that in order to think clearly and make decisions, we need to manage our emotions when they overtake us unexpectedly. Dealing with the Feeling lets us do just that.

Dealing with the Feeling

To balance the emotional part of your inner landscape, try three simple steps before moving to resolve an issue: 1. Spot it. 2. Say it. 3. Okay it.

What do I mean? First, **spot it**—identify the emotion that you are feeling. Literally ask yourself, "What am I feeling?" In the case of the schoolteacher, my answer was fear.

Next, **say** the emotion out loud and expand on it. I said to myself, "I am afraid because my son has ended up with this teacher whom I have not heard good things about."

Finally, **okay it**. That is, validate the feeling. "It's okay for me to feel this way," I went on. "I'm only looking out for my son's best interest."

Now you're ready to solve the problem. If you're stuck, talk out the solution, either in your head or with someone you trust. Either way, by following the three steps above, you will be able to rise above the fog of confusing emotions. Your thinking brain will kick in, and you will be able to think a little more clearly. Then you'll be able to move toward resolving the issue more objectively and less emotionally.

When I put my feelings about Navin's teacher in perspective, I was better equipped to make an intelligent decision about my next step, and that's when my teacher friend came to mind. I had been too emotionally tangled up to have thought about her earlier.

When you complete the three steps—spot it, say it, and okay it—you're turning down the volume of your emotions and inviting your thoughts to participate in the problem-solving process. Dealing with the Feeling helps us manage our inner communication landscape by bringing it back into balance. This simple practice assists us in accessing our innate intelligence, empowering us and leading us to resolve any issue we might face. It also helps us build good, effective communication skills. Dealing with the Feeling is a foundational practice that leads us to the larger goal of building a strong relationship with our kids.

Dr. John Gottman—researcher, emotional intelligence advocate, and author of *Raising an Emotionally Intelligent Child*—and Dr. Goleman have each spent some twenty years working in the EI field. Dealing with the Feeling is my interpretation and expression of their lifelong work of bringing EI and its benefits into the mainstream. Dr. Gottman writes: "In the last decade or so, science has discovered a tremendous amount about the role emotions play in our lives. Researchers have found that even more than IQ, your emotional awareness and abilities to handle feelings will determine your success and happiness in all walks of life, including family relationships."[4]

Once you try Dealing with the Feeling a few times, you will have fast-forwarded yourself into emotional management and into becoming more actively "emotionally intelligent." This simple tool will become like a personal thermostat, helping you turn the heat down and stay cool, even in the midst of the most difficult dilemmas. It will help you respond to situations thoughtfully instead of simply reacting to them; you will be able to confront parenting challenges intelligently by calming down any bubbling emotions and bringing your thinking mind to the forefront.

Just as it is important to manage our emotions in order to fully access our intelligence, it is equally important to manage our thoughts and make room to "feel" our way through situations. Getting caught up in overanalyzing something can leave us feeling stuck on the question of what is right or wrong.

"I am an overthinker," said a dad in one of my classes. "I tend to lean less on my emotions, especially while making decisions. How would Dealing with the Feeling benefit me, considering that my thinking mind is already always in the forefront?"

This father is not alone. Many of us have a tendency to think before we act, sidestepping our emotions in our desire to "do the right thing." In such cases, it helps to turn *up* the volume of your feelings and bring them into the decision-making process—to think "feelingly," as I like to say.

Dealing with the Feeling helps us balance our communication by either:

1. Turning down the volume of noisy emotions so we can consult our thoughts before making a decision, or

2. Turning down the volume of overpowering thoughts so we can check in with our feelings before making a decision.

The more intelligently and consciously we balance our thoughts and our emotions, the more we practice balanced communication, and the more we boost our children's self-esteem—and our own parental confidence.

Confidence is that power that allows us to rely on ourselves, and it underpins effective parenting. If we are confident about the decisions we make, then the comments of others won't disturb us. Honor yourself by believing in the decisions that you make for your family. Remind yourself what an important job you have taken on as a stay-at-home parent or a working parent or a single parent or a parent-to-be. Be proud of your commitment. And when a tornado of emotions or thoughts seems to set you back, know that Dealing with the Feeling will put you right back on track.

So when your spouse asks, "Why didn't you pick up the dry cleaning today?" you will stay calm and respond with, "I had a super-busy day, honey. I'll get to it tomorrow." If you honor your commitments from the heart, when a friend says you're lucky to take in a matinee, you can confidently answer, "Yes, I'm glad that I can stay home with my kids, and I'm lucky that my mom can watch them for me if I need a break," without feeling guilty. And whenever you doubt yourself because of your choice to continue working after you become a parent, you will very quickly validate your choices by dealing with your own feelings, step by step. It will become clear that both things are important to you and that regardless of your work commitments, you always do the best you can for your child. In every case, Dealing with the Feeling helps you take the pressure off and respond with the confidence that comes from within—from your inner perfection.

Remember what Honorable Parenting consists of: First, accept your decision and respect it. And second, balance your inner and outer communication landscapes by Dealing with the Feeling, whether it's fear, anxiety, doubt, or some combination of these. And if you find those negative emotions resurfacing, keep the following affirmation close at hand: *I am an honorable and confident parent doing the best that I can.* Feel the meaning of every word of this affirmation, and repeat it often. Watch how this takes you back to a balance of thoughts and emotions, strengthening you from the inside out, helping you dial in to your Parental Guidance System, your PGS, using your calm and reassuring inner perfection.

Affirmations serve as easy reminders when we've started to drift away from our intentions. Repeated affirmations also strengthen our communication habits. And yes, it does take a little practice, but the good feeling and confidence that follow are well worth the small effort. Even though there are suggested affirmation reminders at the end of each chapter and in the toolbox at the end of the book, feel free to use your own words to write your own affirmations; they are most powerful when they reflect your natural style of speech. Let your affirmations reflect your own personality.

In fact, your entire parenting personality might be different from that of other parents. Even siblings brought up by the same parents may have different parenting styles. And that's okay. Remind yourself that you are "perfect" just the way you are. Our parenting personalities are as unique and perfect as a thumbprint. Why? Because we are as unique as our thumbprints, and so are our kids.

One mom shared that she and her husband had started to set aside Friday as "date night" and added, "Some Fridays, we can't wait to get away from the kids. It makes us feel like we're bad parents." That's hardly true. Let's try Dealing with the Feeling here. Pretend you are this parent. First, *spot it*: Recognize that you are surrounding yourself with emotions like anxiety and guilt. Then *say it*: "I'm feeling anxious and a bit guilty." Finally, *okay it*: If you've had a difficult or even just busy week at work or with the kids, it's no wonder you're looking forward to spending some adult one-on-one time with your partner. How can that be bad? It's okay!

When we take care of and honor our own needs, we are better equipped to take care of and honor our children. Sociologist and happiness expert Dr. Christine Carter, in one of my all-time favorite parenting books, *Raising Happiness*, calls this "putting your own oxygen mask on first." We all need a break! Just because you need a change of scene does not mean that you are ignoring your kids or that you're a bad parent. If setting aside a "date night" works for you, and you are confident that your kids are well taken care of, then that's all that matters. Enjoy your break. Some parents or couples make that time once a week, some once a month, and some only on special occasions. There is no right or wrong here, no good or bad parenting. If it *feels* right, and your kids seem fine, then your PGS is giving you the green signal. Wear your decision confidently!

Parents have asked me many times which style of parenting is best. Every time, my answer is the same: It depends on you, your child, and the situation at hand. Some parents are instinctive; some are authoritative. Some feel that their kids thrive on attachment, others are hands-off, and still others feel comfortable in "helicopter" mode. And some are a combination of all of the above. Trying to follow or identify yourself with one particular parenting style will only lead you to frustration. There are more than 100 million families in the United States alone. How can they all possibly be grouped into just a handful of parenting styles?

Furthermore, being a parent does not require choosing a rigid role. As we will learn in our discussion of the second communication tool, parenting has to be flexible and adaptable. For now, just trust and honor your unique parenting style, and know your style will evolve as you evolve, both as an individual and as a parent. Being honorable, then, is knowing, believing, and reminding yourself that you are the perfect parent for your child. And trusting that when something is not right, your PGS will alert you. You will feel it. Stay tuned in, and listen to those alerts from yourself or your child. This is how you will get more and more comfortable with honoring yourself and your child.

Honoring Your Child

From the moment we hear the news that we are expecting a child, we start preparing, planning, and researching. *Who is the best pediatrician? What is the best formula? Which is the safest crib, stroller, playpen, or car seat? What accessories and toys will my child need?*

Basically, we start educating ourselves. We talk to friends and family, we look up products and read reviews, and we learn from others and their experiences. It's as if someone turned on a switch and sent us into learning mode. We become sponges for information, committed to finding out all that we possibly can about this new phase of our lives. In essence, the simple news of the arrival of our baby makes us more open to learning new things and growing as individuals.

By no means does this learning phase end with the baby's arrival. When this new life becomes part of *our* life, we learn to survive on little sleep, to do what needs to be done, and to give what needs to be given . . . and then some. Our little miracles affect our inner growth as well. There's a popular quotation, "While we try to teach our children all about life, our children teach us what life is all about." How true that is! So while we play this all-important role of teachers in their lives, our children do much the same for us.

Children teach us to be more patient; they teach us to be more responsive; they teach us to be more compassionate and empathetic; they teach us the depth of unconditional love. They refine us, building our character and making us better than we were. They are our soul mates, and it was certainly love at first sight with them—a commitment of a lifetime. The soul mate we marry can become an "ex," but the soul mates we have in our children will be ours forever, until the end of our life. Their presence teaches us much more about ourselves than we ever thought we could know. To top it off, they teach us to expect the unexpected—anytime, anywhere.

We often believe that *we* are the ones taking care of our children. That's true, of course, but our kids also take care of us. They fulfill our human need to feel loved and wanted. They have the power to make us laugh at the silliest little things, the power to make us cry when they are hurt, the power to lift us up with a single hug when we are down. Their mere presence in our life adds new meaning and a new dimension to each chapter of our life. Their very presence inspires us to be better human beings. That is worthy of honor, don't you think?

Remember, honoring your child does not mean you need to put them on a pedestal or forego discipline when necessary—that, too, is part of the parent-child relationship. However, we honor our kids most when, while we guide or discipline them, we give them this gift of unconditional love by accepting them and respecting them for who they are, first and foremost. And if we had the choice to pick any child from a lineup of children, we, too, would pick only our very own. They are just as perfect for us as we are for them.

Accept and Respect

Each child is born into this world with unique gifts—that is, each child has something nobody else has. It could be a whole lot more than others, a whole lot less, or simply a whole lot different. Nevertheless, what our children have is "whole" for them. Deepak Chopra tells us that our "individuality is intimately woven into the fabric of life—that [we are each] a strand in the web of life."[5] Accepting and respecting this uniqueness or individuality is the key to honoring our children and winning their hearts.

Within the heart of our mind and the mind of our heart, we should accept our children just as they are and respect their individual personalities, honoring them for their ability to complement us and one another. Herman Hesse captured this intention in his story *Narcissus and Goldmund*:

> We are sun and moon, dear friend; we are sea and land. It is not our purpose to become each other; it is to recognize each other, to learn to see the other and honor him for what he is: each the other's opposite and complement.

If we keep in mind that we have much to learn from our kids and that they are our perfect complement, we honor their individuality. Of course, honoring our children doesn't mean that we should roll out the red carpet for them. But when we understand and appreciate their role in our lives, we start to move toward acceptance. And when we accept their individuality and their personality, we move toward respect. And respect? Well, that is simply love in action. When we respect our children, we act upon the unconditional love we feel for them.

When my daughter, Nitasha, was two, she could sit in her high chair for an hour and color or make things out of play dough, fully focused. My son, Navin, when he was two, could not sit still for more than five minutes. But when Nitasha got mad, watch out! If she didn't have her way, she would spend half the day with a frown on her face, arms folded, telling everybody, "I'm not your friend." Navin, on the other hand, did not need to always have his way. He could lose a toy, break it, or give it away without much fuss. He was happy to move on to the next thing. The kids were as different and unique at two as they are today. Both have different strengths and weaknesses. As I grew to accept and respect this fact, I felt more empowered to manage their day-to-day issues accordingly.

"I understand that boys and girls are different in their personalities and their interests," remarked a mom in one of my classes, "but I have two boys, and they're completely different!"

"Why would you get two of the same?" responded another mom. "No one does! And if they did, how boring would that be? My sister and I are completely different, and my mom always said that this alone kept her life 'interesting.'"

Yes, life is designed to keep us interested, to keep us changing and evolving. After a certain point, it's all about internal growth. All of life is a flow of relationships and experiences that lead us down this path of growth. If we stop growing, we start to stagnate, and we get stubborn and stuck in our ways. In our careers, our community, our beliefs, and our relationships, we are always "on the grow"—or at least we should be.

Growth, happiness, and communication are all interrelated and dependent on one another. How often have you heard people say they left a job because there was no room for growth and they weren't happy anymore? It's also true in marriage—think about how common it is to blame divorce on a lack of communication, or to say, "We grew apart, and I was no longer happy." As artist John Butler Yeats put it, "Happiness is neither virtue nor pleasure nor this thing nor that, but simply growth. We are happy when we are growing."

By accepting and respecting our kids, we not only make room for that growth in ourselves, we also encourage them to accept and respect themselves, which makes both parent and child feel more content, fulfilled, and happier. And the icing on the cake is that happy parents raise happy kids.

But what is the main ingredient for making kids happy? The answer is simple: For kids to be happy, they have to *feel good* about themselves. That's something we all aim for. Besides our ultimate goal of having a good long-term relationship with our kids through good communication, remember that we also strive toward raising kids to be happy, think positive, and do good. Why? So they can stand on their own two feet and be independent, or as I like think of it, "in-dependent"—that is, dependent on their inner selves. For that, they need confidence. And just as confidence is paramount in parenting, it also plays a huge role in a child's personal success. Confidence helps kids grow, become independent, and feel good about themselves. Confidence ushers in happiness. And we can help give them that confidence by first accepting and respecting them, just as they are.

I say "first" because even when our children are out of line, we must make the effort to accept the situation and to respect their feelings about it. Only then can we lead them to the next step, which is to point out that something they did is unacceptable. If we get stuck on *I can't believe you did this,* then there's nowhere to go. Coming down too hard on kids about a mistake can quickly damage self-esteem and self-confidence and will only cause the child to shut down and shut you out.

That being said, building kids' confidence by helping them recover from mistakes requires emotional management; otherwise, we have just shut the window and not cleaned up the dust. When we accept and respect each child's personality, likes, and dislikes, we honor the child and groom him or her for learning, but we also have to be willing to apply Dealing with the Feeling in order to complete the process. That's part of Honorable Parenting.

Dealing with the Feeling will teach your children to put situations in perspective and will help them feel good about themselves, even when they make mistakes. This is what will build their emotional intelligence, which, research tells us, is a huge indicator of how well our kids will do in the game of life. When we help our kids manage their emotions, we raise kids who are emotionally intelligent and confident. They score, and we score.

Dealing with the Feeling . . . for Kids

"How can I possibly practice Dealing with the Feeling with my two-year-old, who is having a tantrum over wanting a Popsicle right before dinner when she is tired and beyond reason?" a mom asked me. "She does not even know how to put words together. Will she understand or respond to this?"

This is reality parenting, my friends—real issues with real parents and real children in real time. It's one thing for me to advocate Dealing with the Feeling and a whole other ballgame to put it into practice. So let's break down this mother's concerns and address them one at a time.

When a child is tired and unreasonable, the chances of getting through to him or her right at that moment are lower, but it still is worth a shot. Try this:

First, *spot it*. Identify the underlying feeling: She is crying because she is feeling sad.

Second, *say it* out loud: "Are you feeling sad because you don't get to eat the Popsicle right now?" When you put the emotion into words for the child, you are helping her recognize different emotions and building her emotional intelligence vocabulary. You are showing that you understand her, which in itself is a huge "feel good" for the child.

Third, *okay it* by validating it and relating to it: "I understand, love. I would feel sad, too." Validation is the heart of empathy. When you validate your child's behavior, you *accept* how the child is feeling, and you *respect* his or her expression of those feelings. In other words, validation lets your child know that it's okay to feel sad and it's okay to cry to express that sadness. By relating to this sadness, you make your child feel that he or she is not alone and that you understand his or her feelings.

Our feelings are what they are. They are neither right nor wrong. Sometimes we can justify them and make sense of them, and sometimes we cannot. Dr. Christine Carter, whom I quoted earlier, calls this "emotion coaching." When we emotion-coach our kids, we are teaching them to be emotionally intelligent and to manage their feelings and situations. Feelings that are left unmanaged or unaddressed end up hiding somewhere for now, but they are sure to resurface unexpectedly, at some other time. Unaddressed feelings are the primary reason for communication breakdowns between any two people, not just parents and children.

Needless to say, if a child is tired and perhaps "beyond reason," you might have to allow the tantrum to pass before you try Dealing with the Feeling. However, it is important to address it later or the next day, when the child is calmer. For example, you could say, "I know you were feeling sad yesterday when Mommy didn't give you the Popsicle before dinner. I understand how you felt. Mommy would feel sad too."

Then move to the resolution. That next step might go something like this: "Since I understand how you felt, can you try to understand what Mommy felt?" Chances are the child is nodding her head *yes* by now. Continue to explain how you felt, in words and perhaps facial expressions that your child can grasp: "I love to see you enjoy your Popsicles, but Popsicles are fun food, not energy food. And before you sleep, you need energy food to build your muscles and make your beautiful eyes shine—so when you wake up in the morning, you are strong like the trees and shining like the sun . . ." or whatever comes to you naturally. "You can have a Popsicle after lunch today—how's that?"

"Oh, boy, that sounds like a lot of work," said the mom who had raised the issue.

Actually it is less time- and energy-consuming than putting up with and pacifying tantrums, I promise you. Besides, repeated tantrums not only build bad communication habits, they also give stubborn emotions permission to reside in our children's personality. And if these emotions are there too long, it takes a lot more work to undo them and to deal with the frustrations and aggravations that behavioral issues bring to the table, for both parent and child, later on.

What about the second part of this mom's original concern: "She does not even know how to put words together. Will she even understand or respond to this approach?"

Consider this: Does a two-year-old understand that the alphabet is the first step to learning how to read a book? No, of course not. But at two, he or she can start to learn the alphabet anyway. We know that learning to read is crucial to kids' success, and eventually they reap the benefit. We also know that they can learn good alphabet habits early when we make that process fun and when we're repetitive and consistent. Before we know it, our little geniuses go from alphabet recognition to reading words.

Similarly, when we repeatedly introduce them to emotions early on, they'll learn to identify with and recognize those emotions, and before you know it, they will be able to put them in words. It is up to parents to build a child's emotional vocabulary, and that has to be done in a fun and consistent manner, too. With repetition, kids will get it, and pretty soon both parents and children will reap the reward. This is emotional intelligence. Yes, it takes a little practice and consistency. But the benefits of EI, as the research has shown, are priceless. The more you practice, the better kids get at it, the fewer the tantrums and the arguments, and the easier your job gets. This is at the heart of Honorable Parenting.

Emotional intelligence begins with Dealing with the Feeling, and (just as with the alphabet) the sooner you start, the easier it is to teach.

Whatever the age of your child, it's important to use language constructively when you're managing emotions. Try to add the word *feel* to the emotion that you are helping the kids identify. Replace "I know you're sad" with "I know you're *feeling* sad." This is an easy way to help children understand the fluidity of emotions. It helps them learn that emotions are temporary and can be changed. Dr. Daniel Siegel, a clinical professor and psychiatrist at UCLA, calls this "Mindsight." His research has led him to advocate training the mind to see feelings as things that come and go. He writes that mindsight is the "difference between saying 'I am sad' and 'I feel sad.' Similar as those two statements may seem, there is actually a profound difference between them. 'I am sad' is a kind of self-definition, and a very limiting one. 'I feel sad' suggests the ability to recognize and acknowledge a feeling, without being consumed by it."[6]

As kids get older and their emotional vocabulary gets stronger—that is, as they are able to put words to their feelings—parents can segue into asking, "What are you feeling?" and allow the kids to answer the question. Empowering our kids to recognize their own feelings will serve them tremendously in building strong social connections, relationships, and careers.

Even if your kids are older, and this is your first introduction to the concept of EI, it's not too late to teach them. Research into the scientific theory of neuroplasticity has revealed that our brains change dynamically throughout our life. It turns out that our brain has the capacity to reorganize itself, and we're capable of learning at any age. So all parents, with a little effort, can help sculpt their children's brains by being emotionally intelligent themselves and helping their kids follow suit.

Just as we can fill a bucket drop by drop, through Dealing with the Feeling we can build a child's emotional intelligence bit by bit, at any age. And once they are able to understand their own feelings, they will start to have a better grip on their own response. Before you know it, their self-understanding will lead them to understand the feelings of others around them, and they will thrive socially as emotionally intelligent, empathetic, and compassionate children. They will be equipped to put their feelings into perspective and move more freely toward being happy, thinking positive, and doing good for themselves and those around them.

Even though you might not always be able to practice Dealing with the Feeling or be successful with it every time, do it as often as you can. Only with practice can we build positive communication habits. Keep in mind that parenting—and Honorable Parenting—is a practice: The more consciously you do it, the better you get. And when you or your kids make mistakes, honor those, too. Mistakes are meant to be learned from. If we didn't make errors, we would never grow.

One mom I know experienced both sides of this coin and saw the amazing turnaround that Honorable Parenting can create. She started off by complaining about how disconnected she felt from her fourteen-year-old son, who had begun spending time with a girl she did not approve of.

"But why don't you like her?" the son asked.

"I just don't," his mom spat back. "She dresses way too provocatively for a fourteen-year-old." She cut off her son's next question, saying, "I don't need to give you any more of an explanation."

When the boy snuck behind his mom's back, she grounded him. That behavior escalated to the point where he was defiant over everything. Within three months, mother and son were barely talking. The boy's grades had gotten better, though, which confused his mom. Perhaps the extra time that he was spending after school doing homework every day was helping him.

One day after school, the mom ran into his teacher, who also commented on her son's new academic success. When the proud mom complimented her son that evening and asked him what his secret was, he snidely remarked, "What do you care? You don't even like me."

The mom was heartbroken. She blamed the situation on the girl she didn't like. After a class on Honorable Parenting, however, she promised, just for a day, to accept and respect her son's choice and try Dealing with the Feeling. This is how their conversation went:

"I'm *feeling* hurt that you think that I don't like you and that you won't talk to me anymore," she said. "I love you with all my heart. I know you're angry with me because I don't like Jenna. But today I want to know what else you're feeling."

Much beyond her expectations, he accepted her invitation to communicate and responded angrily, "I'm not angry with you because you don't like Jenna. I'm angry because you decided to not like her without even getting to know her."

She took it to the next step and okayed it. "You're right, I see your point."

Her son went on, "How would you feel, Mom, if someone who didn't even know me said that they didn't like me?" He paused. "Do you want to know why my grades have gotten better? Because Jenna's really smart, and we do our homework together after school every day. I've even gotten better at geometry, my worst subject." He continued, "She's fourteen, and she already knows that she wants to be a fashion designer and have her own business someday. She has made me think about what I want to be when I get older. She dresses trendy, not provocative. Do you know that she has never had a boyfriend, and that her parents died in a car accident when she was four? The old lady who comes to pick her up is her grandma."

That exchange was the most that they had talked in a month. The mother was stunned. By making a little effort to open the door to emotional expression, she had given her son the green light to begin a conversation. Now, with the lines of communication open and their feelings expressed, she was able to see things more clearly. Embarrassed by her behavior, she decided to give Jenna a chance and invited her over the next day.

Over the next few weeks, the mom shared her progress with the rest of our class. She and her son were starting to communicate again. She had never dreamed that her fourteen-year-old boy would say, "Thanks for caring about how I feel, too, Mom."

The more we try to control issues, the more they get out of control—especially with older children. Communication is about coming to common ground with your kids. That can only happen if parents start peeling off the emotional layers by initiating the practice of Honorable Parenting: accept, respect, and Dealing with the Feeling. This is what prompts inner growth and uncovers our inner perfection, bridges the gap, and brings parents and children closer.

The mother in my class was able to learn from her mistake and develop an even better relationship with her child. Growth—both ours and that of our children—is dependent largely on how we recover and what we learn from our missteps. If we never made mistakes, how would we learn? A dear friend always reminded me to put mistakes and hurt feelings into perspective: We need to remember that on the larger scale of life, *it is all good*. Tell yourself, "I will be fine and so will my kids," and sooner or later, that will come to pass. After all, their happiness and growth are directly related to yours. So be confident that all is good, and remind yourself and your kids of that as often as you can, especially in down times. After a struggle, it will help speed up the recovery process and encourage everyone to bounce back more quickly. Keeping things in perspective helps all of us feel good, which is a goal of Honorable Parenting.

And if you still have doubts, realize that such feelings are there to help and guide you—as long as you can see through them. Doubt, like any negative emotion, is a compass that can point you in the right direction.

You can minimize doubt through Honorable Parenting, which is a huge confidence booster that helps you first accept and respect yourself and your child, and then apply Dealing with the Feeling to help put emotions and issues in perspective. Honorable Parenting is the first of your communications tools, which are part of your Parental Guidance System.

Granted, we cannot always be free of the proverbial roller coaster of emotions, but Honorable Parenting can return us to balanced communication whenever we stray. The more balanced we are, the more confidently we parent. And we need that confidence to do well the most important job we'll ever do.

The simpler I can make this important job for you, the more fun you will have, and the happier you will be. It follows, too, that your kids will be happier, and they will thrive even more.

The success of our children is not just our own family heirloom; it doesn't benefit us alone. It also affects our children's future families, their community, and the world they will live in. By making habits of these simple, intelligent, mindful communication tools, we draw on our inner perfection. This is how we uplift not only the lives of our children but also those of others in the future. For though, as they say, our children are living messages that we send to a time that we will not see, we can most definitely touch that time by what we do now.

Affirmation Reminder

I am an Honorable and confident parent doing the best that I can. I accept and respect myself and my child just as we are.

Quick Takeaways

- Accept and respect yourself and your child—feelings included.
- The Communication Balance is the balance of your thoughts and feelings (inner communication landscape), which leads to your expressions (outer communication landscape).

Communication Balance

Thoughts + Feelings (inner communication landscape)

Expressions (outer communication landscape)

- Effective communication means balancing your thoughts and your feelings to guide your expressions.
- To fast-forward into balanced and effective communication, as often as you can, practice **Dealing with the Feeling** with yourself and your child:
    - ✓ *Spot it*—identify the feeling (anger, sadness, hurt, etc.)
    - ✓ *Say it*—say the feeling out loud ("I know you're feeling angry.")
    - ✓ *Okay it*—validate it ("I understand how you must be feeling. If my brother broke my toy, I would feel the same way too.")

Now, move to resolve.

Approachable Parenting:
Growing Trust

Stay committed to your decisions, but stay
flexible in your approach.
—*Tony Robbins*

My son's favorite teacher of all time was Miss Dub-T, short for Mrs. Whitlock-Trotter. This wonderful lady was Navin's math teacher all through high school. One day toward the end of freshman year, my son and his best friend, Ro, walked in the door, laughing. "Tell Mom what you said to Miss Dub-T today," said Ro, who was like our second son. Then they both burst out laughing again.

"Hurry up, already," I said, joining in their contagious laughter and thoroughly enjoying the scene. "The suspense is killing me!"

"Okay, Mom, you'll never believe what happened today," Navin finally began. "The bell rang, and we were at the end of math class.

As I passed Miss Dub-T's desk on my way out, she said, 'Hey, Navin. Nice job on your test.' And I answered, 'Thanks, Mom.' The whole class burst out laughing. I said, 'Oops, sorry!' and she answered, 'Don't you worry about it, Navin. What a compliment. I'm flattered.' And we all laughed some more."

Later that evening, with the teacher's comment and my son's laughter still very much in my heart, I said, "Nav, you really are doing much better in math, especially considering that it's much harder than last year. You must love Miss Dub-T. She's that good of a teacher, huh?"

I've never forgotten my son's answer.

"Mom, she's not just a good teacher," Navin said. "She's a great person. I guess that's why I'm so comfortable with her." He continued:

> She's very approachable, easy to talk to. I feel like I can go to her for help even when I mess up. If I'm struggling with something, she never judges me or makes me feel bad. She really listens. If I don't get the problem, she'll explain it in a different way. When I don't do well on a test and I'm bummed about it, she'll say, "That's okay. I don't expect you to get straight As, but I do expect you to do your best. I'm here 100 percent to help you, but it's your job to reach out. No laziness in my class."
>
> She makes reaching out easy. She guides us but doesn't do the work for us. If we goof off or miss a homework assignment, she lets us have it, but she's never insulting. She's cool, but she's also tough enough to keep us on track. I have even gone to her for advice when I was having trouble in my biology

class. She's not just like that with me but with the
whole class! And there are twenty of us!

As Navin was finishing his senior year in college and his academic career, I asked him who his all-time favorite teacher was. His answer: Miss Dub-T. She inspired him and made him a better student in a subject that was challenging for him. She extracted the best out of all her students by being genuinely approachable.

I took careful note of why my son connected with Miss Dub-T. He had pretty much spelled out what I, as a parent, could do to connect with him in a way that worked for him. And if it worked for him, it worked for me! I took the main points and started to interject them into my communication habits with my son. Paying attention to what he was saying helped me understand how he learned best—a gold mine for parents with kids of any age.

If a teacher could earn so much trust and respect from her teenage students—the toughest children to impress—by simply being approachable, imagine how much trust and respect a parent would earn by doing the same.

Like Miss Dub-T, we parents want to extract the best from our kids and see them succeed, whatever their challenges. We all also want our kids to be able to learn from us, constructively and comfortably. As we noted in the discussion of Honorable Parenting, *we are their first teachers.* And if we make ourselves approach-able—that is, if our kids know they are able to approach us—they will turn to us when they need help. If we are there for them, they will depend on us first to help them sort out issues, instead of turning elsewhere.

The world is full of children—teenagers in particular—who are lost, longing for their parents' time and attention. And, yes, they are turning elsewhere. Vanessa Van Petten, a sought-after advocate for teenagers—a "youthologist," as she calls herself—can vouch for that. Through her project Radical Parenting: Parenting Advice Written by Kids, she tries to reconnect parents and teenagers who have drifted apart because of their lack of good communication habits. It is this lack that causes heartache and pain in families and prevents trust from being central to the parent-child relationship. And this lack of communication also plants guilt—an unnecessary weed in our inner communication landscape.

This is exactly why it is my intention, through this book, to empower you with these all-important communication habits. All you have to do is uncover them, recognize them, understand them, and apply them to build on your current parenting practice, making them your very own. The first three steps—uncovering, recognizing, and understanding these habits—will come naturally as you read this book. Applying them, however, calls for your commitment.

The fact is our children want us to be approachable. They are most comfortable and familiar with us, their parents. If we make being approachable a habit from their youngest years, reaching out to us will be second nature to them. And the icing on the cake is that we will have showed them, by example, how to be approachable themselves.

So now let's break down Miss Dub-T's secrets to being approachable: Be available, be flexible, and set guidelines. Following these steps can help us set up communication habits for success. We can allay guilt, doubt, and worry within ourselves while building trust with our kids. When our kids are comfortable about approaching us, we can truly be there for them. When our words and actions say, *I'm here for you*, it strengthens our child's trust in us. And trust is the crown jewel in building a long-term relationship with our kids. Trust lies at the core of the unconditional love that all parents have for their children. Trust showcases the selfless love that often goes unexpressed.

As we explored the "feel good" factor of Honorable Parenting, we groomed our inner landscape with a soil-booster: self-confidence, which minimizes the doubt we feel and express as parents. With Approachable Parenting, it is now time to plant the very first seed—the one that will grow a garden of trust and eradicate the weeds of guilt. That first seed is *time*.

Be Available

Being available is all about time—both *dedicating time* to our kids and *being fully present* during that time. As parents, we already dedicate a lot of time to our kids. Parents and children are always on the clock: *Time to wake up. Time to brush your teeth. Time to get to school. Time to do homework. Time for basketball practice or dance practice. Time for dinner. Time for bed.* That is how we roll.

Parents today are raising their kids in a fast-paced world. "There are not enough hours in the day" is a mainstream complaint. Parents are always trying to get it all done in what seems like a limited window of time. The truth is, we can stretch time as much as we want, and yet there is never enough time to finish everything. Yes, we can take time-management classes and heed the tips to accomplish more in less time. Yet time cannot truly be managed day in and day out.

As I sent my princess off to college, I realized how quickly time had passed. At her high school graduation, I was nothing but pride and joy. I felt that she and I were both ready for this next big step. But when we dropped Nitasha off at school and returned home, not a day went by that first week when I didn't go into her room and shed a tear or two.

How had time just flown by like that? Just yesterday, it seemed, I was changing diapers. Today she is old enough to live alone. How did the years go by so quickly?

A week later, I met a friend whose kids were exactly the same age as mine. Over lunch we talked about how much we missed our newly departed freshmen. Then all of a sudden, my friend went quiet and said, "I wonder if I did a good job? I wish I had spent more time with him. He acted like he couldn't wait to get away from me. All these years . . . I never realized they would go by so fast." Gretchen Rubin, author of the best-seller *The Happiness Project*, is right on target when she says, "The days are long, but the years are short."[7]

You see, when we are in the midst of our busy parenting years, we ask ourselves questions filled with doubt or guilt: *Am I a good parent? Am I doing a good enough job? Am I spending enough time with my kids?* And during these years, we can actually *do* something about it. We can focus on making a change. However, when the kids are grown up and gone, so is that possibility. Since it's impossible to travel back in time, destructive emotions like doubt and guilt may eat at us and be reflected in our relationship with our kids. That alone should make spending quality time with the kids *now* oh-so-important! Quality time is that ingredient that can pacify doubt and guilt while nurturing trust.

I'm not saying you must drop your entire life and spend all your time on parenting. But little by little, you can position yourself now to reap the benefits later. Investing time with your kids in the present is investing in your bond with them in the future. This is like investing in a retirement fund but even more important. When you are younger, it takes some discipline and dedication to put money away every month, but the payoff is security for the future. Similarly, investing quality time with your kids now moves you toward your larger goal of securing and sharing time with them in the future. Parenting is a commitment to grow together, and dedicating quality time now anchors that commitment for decades to come.

Take Five

"But what *is* quality time?" asked a mom in a class on Approachable Parenting. "I am always with the kids, doing things for them as best as I can. I am always spending time *with* them and *for* them. Isn't that quality time?"

Actually, the best quality time is spending time doing nothing except being present. But how do you do nothing with a chatty twelve-year-old girl? Or with a six-year-old boy who probably doesn't know how to do "nothing"?

The answer is to Take Five. Take five minutes a day and dedicate it to nothing—literally, *no-thing*! Tell your child that you will be doing this every day with him or her. For five minutes, sit in your backyard, on your doorstep, by a potted plant on a windowsill—anyplace where you can see nature. Then relax and take your mind off of the rest of your day. This is your one-on-one time with your child, a time when you consciously put away your busy-ness. If you're a pregnant parent, you, too, could (and should) spend five minutes a day with your hands on your tummy, taking deep breaths and just relaxing. If you have more than one child, then make it five minutes per day per child. Have no agenda on your mind, no topics to discuss. If you have something you want to talk about with your child, keep it for another time. This time is meant to be empty, filled only with no-thing.

"But what do I say while we are sitting together?" asked another mom in my class.

If need be, tell your child that you're going to hang out with him or her and just rest. Just sit with your child, put your arm around him, hold her hand, tell him you love him, or ask her how her day was. Do whatever comes naturally to you.

I invariably giggle at parents' responses to this suggestion. We are so used to doing *some-thing* with our kids that the idea of doing nothing seems absurd. But amid the routines of *time to wake up . . . time to do homework . . . time to have dinner,* a five-minute routine of *time to simply be present* works wonders for our relationship with our kids.

"How can I be present when I have a million things on my to-do list?" asked yet another mom.

You can be present by just enjoying the feel of your child's hand in yours, or by just listening carefully to your child and engaging in conversation wholeheartedly. If you have laundry or dinner or work on your mind, drop it. It will still be there later. Your job during these five minutes is to practice being available for your kids. This is what makes you approachable.

And, by the way, you'll also start to see yourself relaxing. To Take Five is a great relaxation technique that lowers your heart rate, regulates your breathing, lowers your blood pressure, increases blood flow to major muscles, reduces muscle tension, improves concentration, reduces anger and frustration, and, to top it off, boosts confidence to handle problems. I didn't make that up. Researchers at the world-famous Mayo Clinic have proven the health benefits of relaxation techniques.[8] So besides benefiting your child, enhancing your relationship, and building trust, to Take Five offers you tremendous health benefits, too!

The goal is to slow down time and perhaps even hold on to it. By being present, we can capture moments that otherwise would have slipped by unnoticed. Bil Keane, the noted American cartoonist who penned the comic strip *Family Circus,* said, "Yesterday's the past, tomorrow's the future, but today is a gift. That's why it's called the present." To Take Five is a gift of time *in* the present.

After her first attempt to Take Five, one mom related her experience of this gift, saying, "It was a little uncomfortable at first." She went on:

> When I told my eleven-year-old that we were going to spend "us" time, just hanging out, she looked at me funny. But she didn't resist. We decided to hang out in our backyard. I heard myself take a few deep sighs, just soaking it in. My daughter noticed this and asked, "Did you have a long day, Mom?" She had never asked me that before.
>
> Then she asked if we were supposed to talk about anything in particular or if I wanted to "discuss" something with her. "No," I reassured her. There was nothing on my mind, but if she had something on hers, I was there for her. She sat for a couple of minutes, and out of the silence came, "Mom, why do I feel like I'm changing?"
>
> I asked her what it was that she felt was changing in her. And the next thing you know, our five minutes of no-thing turned into forty-five minutes discussing puberty! She had gotten wind of the sex-education videos that older students watch at school, and that came up in the talk too. Needless to say, I was shocked . . . and elated. Shocked because I didn't know I had it in me to openly discuss puberty to the extent that I did. I did not

have that kind of relationship with my mother. And elated because had I not taken the five minutes, I would have never known!

I wonder how she would have sorted out all the "embarrassing" (as she called it) questions and feelings that she had. At the end, she even thanked me, gave me a hug, and said she felt much better.

I used Dealing with the Feeling, too. I helped my daughter spot her emotions and put them into words. I told her I could totally relate to her, and it was okay to feel the way she did. That really made her comfortable to keep going. It was pretty incredible. I really feel like we made a huge communication leap.

This is what being available is all about. It means cutting off a phone conversation to dedicate five minutes to doing nothing. It means turning off the TV or putting down the laundry to really listen to what your child is saying or just to *be* with them. It simply means paying attention, which makes your mind available, your perception stronger, and your connection deeper. And of course, as we learned in our discussion of Honorable Parenting, Dealing with the Feeling will always facilitate communication.

It does not matter how old your children are; giving them dedicated time and attention helps parents capture special moments and helps children sort out things that they might have on their mind—all the while growing that garden of trust.

Even four-year-old Saira had a lot to say when her mom tried to Take Five:

"Mommy," Saira said, "I already have a baby sister. I also have a big brother and a big sister"; she had included her cousins. "But can we buy a baby brother?" she added.

"We can't really buy babies, Saira," replied her mom. "We have to ask God for them."

Saira closed her eyes, folded her hands, and whispered her wishes to God. "Okay," she said. "I did it." Immediately she was on to the next thing: "Mommy, do you like 'shushi'?"

"I do," her mom replied.

"Is shushi rice?"

"It's rice and fish."

"Thank you, Mommy. I like that you always help me," said the little one.

Kids are curious and inquisitive. Whether they are teenagers or toddlers, they are always open to learning and growing. If we make it a habit to Take Five with our kids as often as we can, it will become second nature to both them and us. Whether it's a question about puberty, baby brothers, or "shushi," when you Take Five, you open the door and become available and approachable to your kids. You let them know that they can come to you with anything. You encourage them to be comfortable from the get-go, so when the "big" issues come up, talking to their parents is not something new or unusual for them; it is second nature to them.

Quality time would hold even more weight if it happens to be your child's primary "love language," as Dr. Gary Chapman calls it in his award-winning book *The Five Love Languages of Children*. In this brilliant work he and coauthor Dr. Ross Campbell discuss how different children react differently to communication styles and how each child has his or her own primary love language. Quality time is one; the others are physical touch, words of affirmation (encouragement), acts of service, and receiving gifts. Take the free love languages quiz online, and find out the approach that will speak most clearly to your child. You'll be surprised at the grand communication strides you'll make when you use their own love language to communicate with them!

There's no question that to Take Five is a highly effective tool that helps harness quality time, but it may challenge you in practice. Subjects that may come up when you're simply trying to be present could very well surprise you.

"I just spent fifteen minutes with my oldest daughter, age eleven," one mom emailed me after a class on Approachable Parenting. She wrote:

> While doing Take Five, we ended up talking about our frustrations while working together on her math homework. I asked her to explain how I made her feel. She said that she felt she was being pushed too hard to finish her work too fast. She gets mad, she told me, when I accuse her of daydreaming when, in fact, she is trying to remember times-table facts that she can't remember as quickly as other kids can.
>
> She said she feels bad when the same thing has to be explained over and over, and I make her feel worse when I accuse her of not paying attention. She *is* paying attention, she said, but cannot understand something until it is explained a lot of times. She also doesn't like when I take over and start doing the work for her when she really wants to learn and try.

The good part? "In the end," the mom said, "I identified where her anger and frustration over this issue stem from. It really helped both of us to open up to each other, even though it was hard. We understand each other better, and we've promised to make time to talk about our feelings more openly in the future."

The scenario reveals a constructive outcome of applying Take Five. But as all parents know well, not every outcome of such discussions is smooth or constructive. What happens when kids say something we do not agree with? What happens if, when you Take Five, your child touches on a sensitive or sore subject? Well, that's when you remind yourself to take the next step of Approachable Parenting.

Be Flexible

My fifteen-year-old son wanted to play football. I was dead set against it, and he knew it. He begged his dad to let him try out. My husband agreed but forgot to mention it to me—after all, it was only a tryout. Lo and behold, Navin was picked as quarterback. He finally told me when it came time to sign the permission papers to start practice. I refused, and though my husband tried to talk me into it, I held my ground. Even the school headmaster asked me to reconsider, but I wasn't ready to budge. That evening before the first practice, my son came to me and begged me to just listen.

"Okay," I said adamantly, "I'll listen, but I'm not changing my mind."

"Mom, you have always known how much I love football," Navin began. "It would mean so much to me if *you* signed these papers and not Dad. I really want this. You know I'm not an A student. I will never shine with my grades. But I am an A athlete, and this is my chance to shine. Can you please try to understand what it means to me, even though I know you don't like it and you're scared for me?"

It melted my heart to see tears in my six-foot son's eyes. Like any parent, I wanted him to excel every chance he got. For that, I had to look at things from his perspective.

"Let me think about it," I answered, as I hugged him, teary-eyed myself. "Let's talk in the morning." I was surprised by my own willingness to commit to even considering it.

Yes, Navin went on to play high school football for the next three years, leading his team to the conference semifinals and earning other honors. He even went on to play college football for a bit.

Signing those permission papers was one of the toughest decisions I had to make as a parent. I still feel conflicted about it. On the one hand, I got to see him as a true team leader. Football helped make him a responsible and disciplined young man. His grades got better, too, since he knew he had to step up his academics to stay on the team. He learned how to manage his time better. The benefits were priceless.

On the other hand, there was not a single game when my heart didn't skip a beat as those boys got hurt. Bruises, falls, sprains . . . Every game was a challenge for me and a victory for him.

In the end, Navin hurt his back and herniated some disks while playing the sport. My biggest fear of his getting hurt came true, and I badly wanted to say, "I told you so"—but I didn't. The injury forced him to give up football in college, but Navin has no regrets.

As for me, I had to practice Honorable Parenting. I had to honor his feelings and his dreams, even though I strongly disagreed with the path he chose. I practiced Dealing with the Feeling a lot to help me stay strong with my decision to support him, despite my deepest fears about the sport. And I also had to stay flexible—to practice Approachable Parenting—to somehow find it within myself to bend, to bypass my own stance and support what Navin really wanted.

We all will be faced with challenges like that. Our kids will make decisions—right or wrong—that we don't necessarily like, whether it's an activity that we're skeptical about, a girlfriend or boyfriend that we think might not be right for them, or the decision to quit something that they're very good at. All parents come to such crossroads. But unless the decision is clearly detrimental to their existence, our unconditional love will somehow find a way to support them, as hard as that might be.

Whether we like it or not, being a parent requires us to be both naturally strong and naturally flexible—that is, having the ability to bend without breaking. And that can only come from being open-minded. It does not mean being too liberal, however; it just means being open to reconsideration and change.

Think about it: The bedtime of a nine-year-old child is not the same as that of a teenager. But at some point we have to be flexible to make room for that transition. The same is true of decisions about your child's allowance, independence, nutrition, discipline, and responsibilities. These, too, change at different stages of a child's development. If a teenager had only the same privileges at age fifteen as he or she did at age nine, we would be setting our child up for failure. We give our kids more leeway, more freedom, and more of everything as we start to trust them and see that they are capable of handling more. Change is part of growth. And listening facilitates change.

Listening to our kids, hearing about their needs and their wishes— age appropriate, of course—and being open-minded to allow for change is part of the evolution of a parent-child relationship. We have to be creative as parents. We have to redefine, redesign, and refine our parenting skills throughout the different phases of our children's lives. This is all part of being flexible within our parenting role.

Moreover, if we are to be true to our commitment to Honorable Parenting, we have to honor our children's opinions even if we disagree with them. This doesn't mean we have to give in to our kids when they are being unreasonable. It simply means listening to what they have to say. Allow them to make their case and complete their thoughts and feelings—and their sentences, even if you know your answer will still be "no." Sometimes they may have a valid point, and you'll realize that your decisions are due for a change. In any case, listening with an open mind and an open heart supports decision making and complements effective parenting, and helps us be flexible where we need to be.

When your kids are younger, you can help them by making many decisions for them. However, as children grow and mature, encourage them to participate more and more in the decision-making process. The extent to which they can be involved in decision making depends on their developmental level, of course, but even very young kids can and should be encouraged to start making simple choices and solving minor problems. Engage their intellect at any age with questions like, "What do *you* think you should do?" This is a great way to build their communication, resolution, and decision-making skills, well before they approach their more independent teenage years.

Remember that maintaining a balance of thoughts, feelings, and expressions—as we saw with the communication balance "seesaw" in the section on Honorable Parenting—is the very foundation of effective communication. If kids feel that they are being heard and have the freedom to express their thoughts, they will communicate better, make better decisions, and grow to trust us more. This is an integral part of being an approachable parent. Yes, it does require patience, but what good habit doesn't? Whether we are trying to start a new fitness regimen or trying out a new recipe, it's patience that will help us succeed. As the Persian poet Saadi reminds us, "Have patience. All things are difficult before they become easy." Communication habits require both patience and diligence, but their sweet fruits are well worth the effort.

When we show that we are approachable, our children will start to honor us and our role in their lives as well. They will let *us* complete *our* thoughts and will listen to and learn from us through example. If we create a two-way communication environment of accepting and respecting their opinion, they will naturally become open-minded with us and value our opinion. When they disagree with us, they, too, will be up for change; they, too, will be flexible. This type of productive exchange emphasizes the "communing" aspect of communication. It helps them personally and also benefits the social skills and interactions that they are developing beyond their family, with their friends and teachers.

Part of being flexible in problem solving is being creative. A particular approach might work for one child but not another. When issues become repetitive, it's a cue that a creative approach might save the day.

When Nitasha turned six, she began to fuss at her usual bedtime of seven thirty. Every day, for two weeks, it was a different excuse: *My tummy is hurting; I hear noises.* She tried it all. It was time to get creative. Instinctively, I changed her bedtime by a half hour and— without discussing the "fussing" issue—said that now that she was a big girl, she could stay up until eight. It worked! Yes, I had to be flexible about the time, but we were spending a half hour each night catering to her excuses anyway. Being a little creative made the situation better for her and for us.

As you work on being approachable, remember to practice Dealing with the Feeling every chance you get, to build emotional intelligence. Putting feelings in perspective helps both parents and children let their emotional guard down and become more open to listening, learning, and growing. We all know that we can choose different careers, different religions, even different life partners, but we cannot and do not choose different kids. They are ours forever—to nurture, to grow, and to *guide*.

Set Guidelines

Say you have an issue to deal with. You've invested time and effort in trying to reason about it with your child. You've been emotionally intelligent and open-minded and listened to his or her perspective. You've been flexible and creative, coming up with several solutions to help your child manage the problem. Basically, you've been as approachable as you possibly can be. Yet your child is just not getting it. Once again, he or she didn't turn in the homework assignment, for example. Now it's time to draw the line, to lay down the consequences, to send the message loud and clear.

Sometimes parents jump to discipline early on, believing that if they are clear about guidelines from the start, kids are more apt to comply. Other parents let issues repeat themselves before they decide to roll out consequences. In other words, some parents are looser with discipline and some a little stricter. Wherever you fall on that continuum, setting guidelines is a must for children's growth. Guidelines give children direction. They bring clarity to our instructions, and they justify discipline and consequences. Guidelines help children visualize the road map to their own success.

Children usually don't have the capacity to see an end point. A six-year-old entering elementary school is not thinking of high school. An eleven-year-old in middle school is not thinking of college, and a teenager entering high school is certainly not envisioning graduate school or the work force. Younger children are not even able to wrap their heads around the fact that their academic performance in September contributes to how they are going to fare at the end of the school year, especially if they are not doing well or if they are challenged by academics. Parents can see the bigger picture, of course, but kids seldom can. That is why setting small, achievable guidelines is extremely important.

Guidelines are also far better than hard and fast rules. Why? Because rules are rigid, concrete, and, as they say, made to be broken. In other words, rules plant and grow fear, while guidelines demonstrate a love-based approach. Fear and threats create a tug of war between parents and children, and lay out a battle zone that is detrimental not only to your child's progress—and to his or her success and future—but also to your shared relationship.

Yes, rules have to be set when kids are younger to ensure their safety and well-being: *Don't play with fire. Don't touch a hot iron. No sugar before bedtime, no cursing, no electronics in bed.* But as they get older, they outgrow the rules stage; they already know how to stay safe and healthy. Transitioning into *guidelines* will start to pave the road to their independence. Guidelines will help them decide for themselves what is wrong and what is right.

Guidelines give children livable boundaries; rules confine them. Guidelines inspire the productive question "Why?" Rules, meanwhile, prompt children to challenge with "Why not?" Most important, guidelines deepen self-understanding and reasoning. And reasoning helps extract thoughtful responses instead of knee-jerk reactions—a distinction that we'll dive into at length in the section on Reasonable and Responsible Parenting.

As kids get older, tell them that you will recommend guidelines, but it is up to them to follow these. Do lay out the consequences, though. In fact, when you set new guidelines, be clear and consistent about the consequences. This teaches children the cause-and-effect factor of life; it prepares them to take care of themselves when they leave home and readies them to be independent.

At the same time, you have to expect that kids will make mistakes. How else will they learn? How else will they grow? Songwriter Isaac Hayes says, "If you enjoy the fragrance of the rose, you must accept the thorns which it bears." Our kids are our beautiful roses, and mistakes are the thorns that are part and parcel of the ride, both theirs and ours.

Mistakes also offer kids the opportunity to learn and grow, and we all want that for our kids. Sure, they can learn from *our* mistakes, but the real lessons come when they break the rules and challenge the guidelines, just as we once did. Even though we want to protect our kids, to the best of our abilities, we have to allow them to fall sometimes (within reason, of course). By falling and picking themselves up, they will learn that making a mistake doesn't mean it's the end of the world, and they will empower themselves to be resilient and self-reliant.

Needless to say, respecting their parents' wishes and following instructions isn't always easy for kids. If your kids repeatedly defy guidelines, you need to follow through with the appropriate consequences. But why not lean toward *grounding* kids instead of *punishing* them? I know it seems like the same thing, but using specific words can make a big difference in how your kids perceive these consequences. Words have tremendous power; they can confine kids or liberate them. The words we use can either bring kids closer or push them away.

Let's look at those two words a little more closely. The word *punishment* has to do with breaking rules and implies something arduous and grueling. When we steal and break the law, that act deserves punishment. But raising children is an art of the heart. When children break the rules or defy guidelines, they are not criminals. When we soften our words, we allow our kids to lower their guard, which helps them listen better, be more open-minded, and remain less defensive. Grounding not only means losing some privileges, it carries the subtle suggestion that we are actually teaching our kids to stay "grounded."

The other day, I complimented my son on what a grounded young man he had become, and his playful answer was, "How could I not be, considering all the 'groundings' I had to go through?" We had a good laugh, but I found it fascinating that Navin realized the groundings were, in fact, meant to make him stop and think about his actions and how he might approach things differently next time. Even more amazing was that he now appreciated their worth in his life.

Let the Grounding Fit the Deed

When kids misuse computer privileges, ground them from computer privileges, not from a birthday party. If they have misbehaved at a social event, then ground them from another social event. When they break their curfew repeatedly, change their curfew time temporarily. If they have used inappropriate language, make them sit down in a quiet spot and think about what they said and how it affected the people around them. When the grounding matches the mistake, it delivers the message clearly and helps children focus on the issue at hand.

Be prepared for missteps, though. When our kids make mistakes, we need to swallow the impulse to say, "I told you so." Instead try, "I'm not happy with this," and when things have settled down, be sure to add, "but that's okay. What's done is done. What did you learn from this?" Asking that simple question—*What did you learn from this?*—hastens recovery and builds a child's self-esteem. It empowers kids to resolve issues on their own and believe in themselves. It inspires them to learn from their mistakes positively, and with time, it will help them understand the benefits that learning has on growth.

Whenever my son had a big slip-up, my guidelines called for him to take a few quiet minutes to write down what he learned from his mistake—even though he hated to write. Later, when Navin was a college freshman, his first semester was pretty much a total loss. Like many freshmen, he was distracted with everything under the collegiate sun, and my "sonshine," as I called him, was dropping classes left and right. Of course, we didn't realize this, and since we weren't there to catch him, he had to experience the fall and catch himself.

When Navin came home for spring break that freshman year, he seemed really down one day. I asked him what was up, and he said, "I just need to think a little, Mom. College is harder than I thought it would be." He was up late that night, talking to his sister, and I assumed he was sharing what was on his mind.

The next day he seemed better, and that night after dinner, he told us he wanted to talk. He rolled out the actual number of classes he had dropped and failed. My husband's eyes started to pop out of their sockets. I could tell what he was thinking: *The money we spent on tuition could have funded another mortgage!* Then Navin pulled out the handwritten list he'd made the night before. It showed what he had learned from his mistakes. Here are some of the contents:

1. Consistency—It is much easier and less stressful to be consistent with my assignments than to try to play catch up.

2. Value for money—I'm going to get a job so I can understand how hard Mom and Dad work to make the money that I have wasted.

3. Time management and focus—I have to manage my time better and remind myself that my main aim for being in school is to graduate with a business degree so I can fulfill all my dreams of being successful.

Navin had hated making those *What did I learn from this mistake?* lists, especially in his teenage years. But he knew it was a tradeoff. If he made the list, the grounding would be the bare minimum. Many times I even specified a sliding scale: *If you do not make a list, you will be staying home for the next two weekends. If you make a list, you will only miss your friend's birthday party this Friday.* Navin hated writing out those lists, but he did it. And today, when he falls hard, he still does it on his own.

As important as setting guidelines is following through with consequences. Parents in my classes frequently express the same lament: Follow-through is one of their biggest challenges, and more often than not, kids pick up on that.

My sister, for example, was inconsistent with following through on her decisions and much to her dismay, she knew it. Her work schedule changed so often, it meant that each day was also different for her kids. One morning, as she was driving the kids to school, her personal "pinch point" manifested itself as she overheard her kids whispering in the backseat. Her five-year-old, who had seen the iPod in his seven-year-old brother's backpack, said quietly, "You'll get into trouble—Mom grounded you from your iPod until tomorrow!"

Their nine-year-old sister joined the conversation a bit more loudly. "Don't worry," she said, "Mom always forgets about the grounding by the next day." Funny, but true for so many parents . . . and it made my sister realize she needed to be more consistent with the consequences she doled out.

Our children know our strengths and weaknesses just as well as we know theirs. If we don't follow through on our word, they'll learn exactly when and how to work around us. Following through and being consistent with our guidelines and groundings sends a clear message about consequences, just as we send a message about reliability when we promise something to our kids and we live up to it. In both cases, knowing that we will live up to our word builds trust between parent and child.

Parenting is a directorship, not a dictatorship. Our job is to direct our children toward right and wrong, not to dictate every action. If we direct them, we practice Honorable Parenting and Approachable Parenting, which will surely earn us their respect and their trust. However, if we dictate rules, we are doing a disservice to them and to ourselves. We are wasting our time and theirs by keeping them from being independent, and we will still carry the heavy baggage of guilt, doubt, fear, and worry. Most of all, we will drift further away from our larger goal of building a good relationship with them.

With our parenting world in constant flux, follow-through and consistency are among the most challenging tasks we encounter as parents. But our job is to do the best that we can, as often as we can—leaving room for mistakes and for growth from mistakes. There's no reason to feel guilty about a mistake; guilt is unnecessary anger directed at ourselves, and it prevents us from learning. Reminding ourselves of that can help put it in perspective. Instead, take a deep breath and ask yourself the same thing you ask your kids: "What have I learned from this?"

When you practice Approachable Parenting—being available, being flexible, and setting and following through with guidelines—the trust between you and your child will begin to be firmly planted. The more you practice this tool, the more deep-rooted trust will be.

• • •

Honorable Parenting and Approachable Parenting are both tools that help shift our *inner* communication landscape, balancing our thoughts, our feelings, and our expressions. As you apply these tools and make them habits, you will not necessarily alter how you parent right away. What *will* start to shift for the better immediately, however, is your parenting perspective. A relaxed and confident perspective is all you really need in order to strengthen your *outer* communication landscape—the physical connections with your kids, through words and actions.

This connection between the inner and outer communication landscapes—combined with your parental instinct—is what balanced communication and effective parenting is all about. This is the art of parenting with heart.

Using these internal communication tools as our foundation, let's now move forward to Sensible Parenting: using our physical senses to connect with our kids and continue this cycle of parenting at its best.

Affirmation Reminder

I am an Approachable and trusted parent. I listen with an open mind and an open heart, guiding my children and empowering them to learn and grow from their mistakes.

 Quick Takeaways

- Take Five. Give yourself five uninterrupted minutes each day to do nothing with your child. This is the ultimate communication reset tool.

- Be flexible and creative. Listen with an open mind and allow your children to complete their thought. Be open to change and growth, and your children will learn to do the same. If you're not getting through to your child, try a different approach.

- Set guidelines instead of rules. This encourages structure and engages children's intellect and decision-making skills, which fosters independence.

- Let the grounding fit the deed, and, as much as possible, be consistent and follow through.

- Encourage children to make a "What did I learn from this mistake?" list. It helps recovery and growth.

Sensible Parenting:
Nurturing Connections

> Too often we underestimate the power of a touch,
> a smile, a kind word, a listening ear, an honest compliment,
> or the smallest act of caring, all of which have the
> potential to turn a life around.
> —*Leo Buscaglia*

Rewind back to when you became a parent for the very first time. Remember how we gazed into our children's eyes. Remember how we listened so carefully to those coos and cries to figure out what the baby was trying to "say." Remember how we soothed them with a lullaby and how we spoke to them in whispers and soft tones. Remember how a quick sniff told us they needed a diaper change. Remember how they stopped crying as soon as we picked them up. They knew our touch, our voices.

Science confirms that children even know the scent of their parents, especially of their mothers. How sensitive they are! And how perceptive we were! Our ability to use our senses, to be sense-able or sensible, was at its best. We quickly learned the language of our children's senses and used the sensory gifts of our inner perfection to understand them and connect with them. This is what science calls "bonding": the end result of the optimal use of our senses, and the start of our relationship with our kids.

Throughout the first year of raising a child, our sensory communication with our children gets stronger and stronger. The look in their eyes, the tone of their cries, their food preferences, and their facial expressions and body language all become a mode of communication—a first, wordless language—that we clearly comprehend and respond to. Our eyes, our ears, our nose, our voices, and our touch are most active and synchronized with theirs during this stage.

As our children's world expands and they start to interact independently with their environment and develop socially, that first sensory language has to make room for words, which soon become their primary language of communication and connection. Simultaneously, parents start to return to their other responsibilities, as well as managing kids' after-school schedules of sports, music lessons, clubs, art classes, tutoring . . . The list goes on and on. Slowly but surely that first language of unspoken connection between parent and child starts to lag. Instead, instruction and direction through words takes precedence.

Today, more than ever before, we are living in a world of external sensory overload. We are bombarded from every direction by TV, social media, and handheld mobile and gaming devices. Computer screens and the web are practically universal. This sensory overload busies our physical senses and taxes their ability to function well, threatening to overpower their tremendous value in building lasting communication habits.

Cris Rowan, a pediatric occupational therapist who has researched and written about the impact of TV and the web on children's neurological growth, notes that:

> Children's developing sensory, motor, and attachment systems have biologically not evolved to accommodate this sedentary yet frenzied and chaotic nature of today's technology. The impact of rapidly advancing technology on the developing child has seen an increase of physical, psychological, and behavior disorders that the health and education systems are just beginning to detect, much less understand.[9]

Put simply, children are spending a lot of time focused on technology, and although learning to work with it early on has its benefits, the trade-off is huge. Research is pointing to one conclusion: The more extended time children spend with technology, the more disconnected they will become with parental and social communications. This only intensifies: The less they listen, the less they see, and the less physical connection they have, until eventually communication habits weaken, too.

This controversial issue makes Sensible Parenting all the more important. And although this problem seems daunting, the solution is literally at the tips of our fingers. All we have to do is, first, understand and reconnect with the gift of our senses. Next, we must use our senses to activate our Parental Guidance System and develop better communication habits with our kids. That is precisely what the third tool, Sensible Parenting, will help you do.

You will also see, with the backing of new scientific findings from cutting-edge research in positive psychology, how awareness and understanding of your innate senses can help you use those senses as access points to communicate with your kids throughout their life.

From the inner landscape of Honorable Parenting and Approachable Parenting, then, let's now move out to the interactive space between parent and child, through the use of the five channels we call the five senses. It is through these five channels that we make "sense" of the world around us, and it is through these channels that we connect with ourselves and those around us. Our sensory experiences can either deepen relationships or weaken them; we can use our senses to bridge distances and create intimacy—or to build barriers that prevent it.

How annoyed do we get when we are speaking to our kids and they're not looking at or listening to us? How often has a spouse, friend, or family member pretended they were listening when you knew they weren't? The other day I started to talk to my husband about a family issue while he was in the midst of watching a TV show. He turned off the volume, but his eyes were still on the screen. He kept saying, "Uh-huh," in response to my dilemma, but at some point, I realized he was not listening. "What did I just say?" I asked. Of course, he had no clue!

Haven't we all experienced that moment? How disrespected and detached we feel when our senses are denied that connection!

When we look and watch carefully, however, we see things that we might have overlooked otherwise. When we listen with care, we can truly hear what the other is saying. When we choose tasteful words, we get the point across. Sometimes we can even "smell" a situation ahead of time, which helps us be more perceptive and ready to respond. And last but not least, by simply giving a hug, holding a hand, or rubbing an arm, we can touch another's heart and even the soul. Our senses are the vehicles of love itself.

"Love is the poetry of the senses," said French novelist Honoré de Balzac. Sure enough, through the proper and delicate use of our senses, we can recite the poetry of love to those we love most—our children. Through our senses, we can actually access their hearts—their very core. Through our senses, we can build self-confidence, self-worth, and self-esteem in younger children and tear down the walls of self-defense and resistance in older children. By using senses, theirs and ours, we can help break open the cage of emotional mind games and, well, bring us back to our senses. We can use our senses to make sense of things.

Harnessing the use of your senses to pull your heart into the art of parenting is what Sensible Parenting is all about. At a class at the University of Philosophical Research in 2013, I was amazed to learn from health and happiness expert Dr. Jay Kumar that the electromagnetic frequency of the heart is 10,000 times stronger than that of the brain—and that the heart sends electrical signals that the brain then translates into cognitive thoughts.

Contrary to what was traditionally believed, says Dr. Kumar, the brain appears to take orders from your heart, not the other way around. As he points out, "In many ways, science now affirms the adage [about] how important it is to follow your heart."

In other words, the heart is at the center of the psychology of an individual, and it opens the doors to communication. If the heart is calm and happy, the brain will naturally be more relaxed and able to facilitate balanced communication between parent and child.

"Isn't that what Dealing with the Feeling does too?" asked a mom in one of my parenting classes.

Exactly! It calms the emotions and soothes the heart. It takes the burden of unacknowledged emotions off the heart and makes the situation more . . . light-hearted, if you will.

There is no way you can get through to your child without first turning down the emotional temperature. Using your senses is a physical, tangible way to make this happen—an accompaniment to Dealing with the Feeling. Once our sense organs receive stimuli from the outside, we have an internal reaction both in feeling and in thought. That triggers a response or an expression. For example, if we hug or touch our crying child, within seconds he or she starts to calm down and feel better. And that, in turn, makes us feel better, too. What a sensible thing to do!

So while you are talking with your children and helping them handle their emotions, look into their eyes, listen carefully and let them complete their sentences, use a gentle and respectful tone of voice, and rub their backs to soothe their tears. These are all ways to help both parent and child start making sense of the situation.

Use your senses together, or focus on one at a time—whatever comes naturally—and you'll see how *sensible* you feel as a parent. Using your senses mindfully is empowering, and it puts you back in the driver's seat!

Sensible Parenting serves not just to resolve issues but also to deepen connections with your kids, by reintroducing their first language—the silent language of the senses. You can use the calming effects of your senses to help manage daily concerns and enhance communication, just as you did when they were little. So your senses are yet another way to bring balance into communication, first with your feelings; then with your thoughts; and finally, as a result of the two, with your expressions—as we saw in the illustration on page 38. Sensible Parenting leads you right back to better communication with your kids!

And here comes the fun part: Each of our senses has the power, positively or negatively, to stimulate one or more traits of our inner perfection—love, self-confidence, self-esteem, self-worth, and self-respect. With the support of science, let us now explore our senses individually.

Sight—a Connection Beyond Words

Our eyes facilitate vision by bringing in light—by *enlightening* us. Through our eyes we can brighten the darkest of feelings and situations. And even though our eyes are a silent sense organ, they speak volumes. Sad eyes, happy eyes, mad eyes—all are mirrors of our emotions. As Charlotte Brontë wrote in *Jane Eyre,* "The soul, fortunately, has an interpreter—often an unconscious but still a faithful interpreter—in the eye."

When children are little, they say a lot through their eyes, and parents can easily pick up on their child's mood through eye language. When my daughter, Nitasha, was four and she got mad, she would start by squinting her eyes; then she'd tilt her head, fold her arms, and say, "I'm not your friend." It didn't take us long to pick up on her cues. The moment she squinted her eyes, my husband would say, "Uh-oh, here it comes. She's not my friend!" When my son was angry at that age, however, he would sit in a corner, fold his arms, and close his eyes, as if he were trying to hide his feelings.

"Why do you close your eyes when you are mad?" I asked him once.

"Because I don't want to talk to anybody when I'm mad," he said.

"If you don't want to talk, all you have to do is close your mouth, not your eyes, don't you think?" I asked.

"No," he answered, "because when you're sleeping and your eyes are closed, no one talks to you." Basically, Navin was using his closed eyes as a silent language to tell us, *Not now. I'm not ready to talk about it.*

An anonymous quote puts it well: "Look into my eyes and hear what I'm not saying, for my eyes speak louder than my words ever will." If we look carefully, we can easily see what our children's eyes are saying. Then our own eyes can respond accordingly. Although we exchange feelings most often through words, our eyes offer the strongest and deepest form of nonverbal communication. No surprise, then, that this translates into strong connections with our kids.

"When my youngest daughter is mad at me, she does not speak a word," said a mom who was discussing her five-year-old. "She does it all with her eyes. If looks could kill, I'd be long gone." When asked how she responded to that, the mom answered, "Usually, if I'm mad, too, I'll just give her that look back and walk away until I've cooled down enough to talk about it."

Of course! Why use words and add fuel to the fire? Nonverbal communication is a powerful tool that can help resolve issues, and our eyes are its driving force.

The mom went on:

> Just the other day, she had a little outburst when I turned off the TV and told her it was time for bed. Then she gave me her angry-eyes look and just sat there with arms folded. I matched her angry eyes, hand-signaled *Into your room, now,* and walked away. My daughter burst out crying.
>
> Immediately, my heart sank, because I knew she wasn't feeling well, and I'm sure my eyes must have shown that I felt bad. I went to hold her, and after a minute or two, she said, "Your eyes are nicer to me when I'm crying. I don't like your angry eyes. And I know you don't like my angry eyes either!"

> I sometimes feel as though she and I resolve a lot
> of issues in a much quieter way than I could with
> my older kids, because she's very dialed into eye lan-
> guage. It's really kind of nice.

This mother instinctively recognized the power of nonverbal communication with her child. Even so, she doubted herself, wondering,
"Should I be asking her to express those feelings in words instead?"

For a child, learning to express feelings in words and to build an
emotional vocabulary is very important. This is what makes kids
more emotionally intelligent. But you can't ever replace eye language
with verbal language. You can't ask kids to not "look" angry. Those
facial expressions are also a way of communicating.

In 2004, world-renowned technology wiz and entrepreneur Dr.
Roel Vertegaal conducted research to prove a direct link between eye
contact and communication. He concluded that eye contact leads to
increased conversation and problem-solving ability.[10] And in 2013,
Michigan State University released another study confirming his
findings, saying that eye contact "shows attentiveness and interest"
and asking that we consider "using eye contact to show empathy,
concern for others, to manage feelings or to help with communication. Those are all life skills that youth will grow and develop as they
mature into successful adults."[11]

We can definitely use our eyes to balance a child's emotions, even
before we start using words. When their eyes show sadness, we can
use our loving look to comfort them. When their eyes are mad, we
can use our understanding look before we console them. When their
eyes are mischievous, we can use our *"better-watch-out"* look before
yelling at them. At times we can see in our kid's eyes what they are
not saying. "I could just tell from the look in her eyes that she was
hiding something" is something parents often say.

When there is a conflict and your kids are defending themselves or telling their side of a story, put aside all distractions and take a moment to make eye contact with them. Keep your eyes as neutral and emotionless as possible; try not to form an opinion or prepare for a response. This will help show that you are keeping an open mind and being approachable, and it is the most effective nonverbal way to truly honor your child.

In essence, making eye contact lets your children see that you acknowledge, listen to, and understand their point of view. As renowned children's author Kristyn Crow says, "Eye-to-eye gaze between two individuals sends the subconscious message, 'I see you, I want to understand you, I care about you.'"[12] That's a big message for two little eyes to carry, but how well they do it!

Our eyes are called "the windows to our soul" for a reason. Take a peek, parents. Look through your eyes into theirs and you'll be able to see and feel their thoughts and feelings—their inner communication landscape. And through your eyes, show your children *your* inner landscape—how much you love them. Through eye language, you can make a connection beyond words. Through eye language you can and will touch your children's hearts and souls.

Hearing—Expanding the Mind

When my kids were younger, they often complained that I was interrupting their side of the story. They would say, "Can you please at least listen to me and let me finish before you say anything?" So I tried. As I started practicing verbal control, I realized that my kids were right. I almost never *really* listened. I started to notice how quickly my thoughts and my words wanted to jump into their story, well before they were done telling it.

A few years ago I was taking an online class in which spiritual author Eckhart Tolle addressed the topic of listening. By letting kids complete their story, he said, by *really listening* to them, we allow them to complete their own thoughts, which helps them resolve issues on their own. Isn't that what a parent wants? Wouldn't it be great to watch our children resolve their own issues while we listen?

Two days after the class, Navin, then sixteen, walked in the door, very upset at his football coach, who had decided to give a new teammate an opportunity to start in an upcoming game. Competitive quarterback that he was, my son was not pleased by this news. He vented for about five minutes while I made eye contact and listened to every word. Every time I had the urge to jump in, I murmured, "Uh-huh" and "Hmmm" and "Oh," actively practicing what I had just learned. I was determined not to offer my opinion until my son asked for it.

I took a deep breath a couple of times, which kept me from interrupting his story and really helped me to be present, patient, and focused. At the end of his story my son said, "I was still really upset driving home, but I now realize I can't let this bring me down. This is a test for me. If I get worked up about this, my team will pick up on it and feed off of me. I'm the leader of the team, Mom. I can't do that."

At this point, it hit me: He was talking to himself and figuring it out on his own. I continued to "Hmm" and "Uh-huh," thrilled about the direction he was taking.

"I'm just going to go out there on Saturday," Navin concluded, "and do the best job I can for my team, even if I do it from the sidelines. If I'm truly a better quarterback, my sportsmanship will shine on its own."

I was teary-eyed by then. I had watched my teenage son move from angry to rational to constructive. And I hadn't even contributed a word. My six-foot-two-inch son stepped toward me, gave me a hug and kissed my cheek, and said, "Thanks for listening, Mom. Talking it through really helped me figure it out. You're the best," and headed to his room.

I had done nothing. I just looked and listened, offering him silent, uninterrupted space, which helped him resolve the issue on his own. The best part was that I would not have guided him any differently, yet listening had definitely been easier than participating in the conversation.

I also realized that Navin had not really been looking for my opinion. He had merely wanted to vent and share his feelings while he was sorting out the issue in his own mind. He had just wanted to talk it out. And I had allowed that, with no interruptions, which let him resolve things on his own. What's more, for being silent and consciously listening, I'd received a priceless gift: a hug and kiss. Win-win for sure!

That was a new beginning for me in my communication with my teenage son. As I listened more, he hung out with me more, and I know it's because he felt more honored, respected, and appreciated. I had become more approachable by doing nothing other than mindfully listening. I realized that mostly what our kids want is for us to just hear them out as they share their feelings and their stories. I started to do the same with my daughter, who was away in college by then. Every time she called home to discuss a dilemma, I made a conscious effort to fully listen until she was done; I waited for a *What do you think?* before offering my guidance. She, too, started calling home to discuss issues more often. Mostly, a listening ear is all our children are reaching out for. And what comes out of it is the priceless bond of friendship and trust.

Dr. Mark Goulston, a prominent psychiatrist and author of *Just Listen*, wrote in a *Huffington Post* article, "Caring comes not from what *you* say to your child, but [from] what you enable *them* to say to you that's weighing on their minds, hearts, and souls, and then how you hear them out so instead of their feeling dismissed and not worth your time, they feel understood, feel *felt*, feel less alone, and feel worthy."[13]

Understanding this difference between hearing and listening was a huge milestone for me personally. I've come to understand that while *hearing* is merely the perception of sound, *listening* means paying careful attention to both the sound and the source. We have to tune in to the feelings behind the words. As I practiced doing that with my children, my husband, my parents, and my coworkers, I realized how much sharper I was becoming as a mom, a wife, a daughter, and a leader. In fact, listening built not just my children's self-confidence but also my own.

Striving to listen also enhances self-control, and self-control teaches us patience. Being a good listener has definitely made me more patient. And patience has a way of putting us back in the driver's seat—not in control, because we really don't want to "control" our kids, but definitely in the lead, when and as needed.

When your child tells you a story about something that happened in school or with a friend, start tuning in with your senses, one by one. First, make eye contact. Then focus on your ears, and start listening word for word. If you notice your mind drifting, slowly inhale and watch how that helps you tune in again. Taking a slow breath helps you tune back in; you will feel your mind opening and expanding, too—a huge help for parents during a kid crisis. This mindful listening helps us be honorable, approachable, and sensible all at once! If you feel the urge to say something, use neutral sounds and nondirectional words like *Hmmm, Uh-huh,* or *Really*—whatever comes to you naturally. Give your opinion or comments only if it is truly necessary, especially as children get older and are more able to work things out for themselves.

One of the moms in my class tried mindful listening with her teenage son, and the first thing he said after he'd told his story was, "Are you okay?"

"Of course, why do you ask that?" she asked.

"Because you didn't tell me what I should do. Aren't you interested, or don't you care?" he said sarcastically, not knowing how to handle his mom's new response.

"The opposite, in fact," she replied. "I learned that if you truly listen and let your children complete their stories, without interrupting, you help them resolve issues on their own. And that helps build communication and relationships between parents and children."

"Wow," said her son. "I like this. It feels good for me, too. Thanks, Mom." A second later, he turned back and said, "You should take Anthony's mom to those classes with you. She *never* listens! All she does is keep talking over him. He hates it. He doesn't even talk to her about anything important anymore."

What is important to kids might seem little to us, but *everything* is important and urgent to them. The only way we can help them put a situation into perspective and make sense of it is by mindfully listening to them. When we make eye contact and listen closely to what our children say to us—even when it is minor—we exemplify an essential communication habit. Our children feel as though their voices and opinions are heard; they feel as though they matter. This builds their self-worth and self-esteem.

Remember, our ears are not just organs of hearing but also of balance and equilibrium. Mindfully listening to our kids helps us balance their feelings and their thoughts. Mind you, listening does not always have to mean agreeing. It simply means giving them an opportunity to say what's on their mind, without interrupting.

And if we want our children to listen to us, we must listen to them.

That is how we can support them. Mindful listening lets our kids know that our minds—and our hearts—are open to them. It lets them feel the love that we have for them.

Smell — the Nose Knows

I was seven years old when I took a terrible fall at school. My parents could not be informed since we did not even have a home phone at the time. The school nurse, the principal, and my next-door neighbor, who was also a teacher at my school, rushed me to the hospital. The doctors did what was necessary. A few hours later, with my twice-fractured nose bandaged, the same team took me home and delivered me to my mom.

My parents have shared this story hundreds of times. My mother, who burst out crying when she saw me, says she still remembers the strong smell of blood and alcohol from the dressing on my nose. And when she volunteered at a hospital thirty years later, that familiar smell immediately turned her stomach. As for my dad, he would always say, "The second I walked in the door, I could 'smell' something was very wrong! You were sleeping in the other room, and I didn't even see you, yet I knew it. Even before I saw your mother's face, I smelled trouble!"

I was able to understand my mother's reaction years later, in high school, when I studied the connection between smell, memory, and the limbic (emotional) brain. It's true that a certain smell can bring back memories and trigger certain past emotions. But my dad's words about "smelling trouble" always made me giggle.

We hear other such phrases from time to time. "You can smell fear in the air," say news reports of a financial crisis or a natural disaster. We also smell "love in the air," typically in spring. I always wondered if terms like that were merely figures of speech or if there was some truth to them. Does our sense of smell tell us more about the world around us than we think it does?

In November 2012, researcher Gün Semin and his colleagues at Utrecht University in the Netherlands released a study that validates those sayings: They collected sweat from male subjects who had watched a "scary" movie or a "disgusting" one. Then they brought in female subjects who were told that they were taking a visual test. While the test was being conducted, researchers placed the armpit sweat samples in the area so the women would be exposed to them unknowingly. Across the board, those who were exposed to the "fear" samples had a wide-eyed response to the visual test; the women exposed to the "disgusting" samples responded to the visual test with a grimace.[14] Indeed, the nose knows!

I got further, if informal, evidence when a perceptive friend "smelled" trouble and called to get some advice about a situation with her daughter. Here is her story:

> My fourteen-year-old daughter asked me twice in the span of fifteen minutes when I would be taking her younger brother to his soccer practice. She knew I almost always stayed to watch practice. I don't know how or why, but I could actually "smell" trouble. I even had a funny taste in my mouth. I quietly picked up the phone and called a neighbor who lived one street over. Her son was on the same team, and she said she would be more than happy to take my son to practice along with hers. I unlocked the back door and then left the house as usual, and after dropping my son off with her, I parked my car some four houses down, in a spot where I could still

see the entryway to my house. Then I slid low into my seat and almost covered my face with my big straw beach hat. I'm a really stellar detective when I need to be!

Within seven minutes, a tall, skinny kid walked up to my house, and my daughter met him at the door. She knows she's not allowed visitors—especially boys—when I am not home. I snuck into my backyard, got in through the back door, and busted them! I was furious, but thankful that I was right on. I swear, that smell of trouble really heightened my perception and helped me respond.

Our sense of smell helps us perceive otherwise imperceptible information and enhances our sixth "knowing" sense. Like radar, our nose can identify and pick up emotional signals lingering in the air. What happens when we "smell" fear? Our nostrils flare, which makes room for more air, and we start breathing heavily. The same thing happens when "love is in the air." Our heartbeat increases, and we start breathing more deeply.

Breathing is the other important function our nose performs. And how important that is! The air that our nose inhales brings oxygen to our brain, calming our nerves in preparation for a productive response.

The Air We Breathe

The air we breathe is one of the two most abundant and accessible fuels we can draw on to activate our Parental Guidance System and mobilize the communication habits that we are exploring in this book. (We'll cover another such fuel—water—in the section on taste.) Air pumps us up and helps us get back to speed, just as it does a flat tire. The difference is that we actually have to stop and pump air into a tire, whereas we have air to breathe at our disposal anytime! It is an ingredient that our internal organs need to function. Our "know-it-all" nose oxygenates our brain and sharpens our knowing, both consciously and subconsciously. So much versatility in one sense organ! Why not use our nose, mindfully and consciously, to our advantage?

When your fourteen-year-old daughter has snuck her boyfriend into the house, if you react emotionally and offensively, the child will follow suit and react defensively, which will cause her to either shut down or explode. This reaction will get you nowhere. If anything, it throws you back a few steps.

"What do you suggest I do?" snapped my friend. "I was fuming. There's no way I could get myself to pretend I was calm and say, 'Oh honey, come on, let's sit down and talk about this.'"

That's not what I'm suggesting by any means. I believe in discipline. Kids need guidance and structure as they learn right from wrong, and it is our job to deliver this foundation. That's what makes us effective parents. But taking a few deep breaths before you do anything else can help you get to that constructive conversation sooner rather than later. Usually we blow up, then our kid blows up, and we all say hurtful things to one another, which adds to the emotional damage and baggage of feeling guilty and bad. Why add fuel to the fire when we know the damage it can cause?

So as parents, how do we usher in emotional control when we are about to blow up? By paying attention to our breathing.

In the midst of anger and fear, try taking five deep, conscious breaths, inhaling the air through your nose and into your belly and your brain. Watch how your emotional temperature drops. Attentive breathing is a powerful habit that brings communication into balance by deflating the burden of emotions, making room for the intellect to participate, attentively guiding our words and actions toward effective parenting.

"I thought this would be really hard for me," said one mom in my class, shortly after we had explored the potential of the five senses and their role in Sensible Parenting. "But much to my surprise, it worked." She had been angry at the words and tone of voice her husband used with their son, after the principal had called to say their boy had pushed another seven-year-old on the playground:

> I felt like a fool, inhaling and exhaling profusely, pacing back and forth to calm my anger. But I was determined to try to calm his anger with respectful words. And had I not taken those five deep breaths, I would have gotten into a fight with my husband. Then I would have had a separate issue on my hands.
>
> Those five deep breaths gave me the patience to wait until after my son was sent to his room, to speak—not scream—at my husband. I was firm, though. Miraculously, I found myself saying, firmly but calmly, "When you use words like that, you hurt his feelings, which will actually make it harder to get the point across to him, don't you think?" My husband just stared at me and said, "You're right. How can I get the point across when he's crying like that? I was just really mad. I'll go talk to him."
>
> I was stunned! Those five breaths not only calmed me; they calmed my husband, too. Ten minutes later, he walked out holding my son's hand, and my son

said to me, "I'm really sorry. I should not have pushed him back. I should have told the teacher."

As he went to do his homework, I pulled my husband aside and said, "Pushed him *back*?"

"Yes," my husband said. "I'm going to school tomorrow. Evidently, he got pushed first, but nobody saw it. Had you not calmed me down, I wonder when we would have found out . . . if at all."

The calm and comfort of the five breaths this mom had dared to take at that moment actually reached her son through his father. And when the dad went to school the next day, he was right: Their son was not entirely at fault.

Mind-body medicine research has validated the stress-busting, calming, and healing effects of deep breathing on both mind and body. When we are calmer, we are better communicators, and our kids will learn to follow suit. It will become second nature to them.

Above all, we should recognize that air has incredible power and potential. It can lift a delicate, soaring bird or a huge airplane. It is a resource of great energy for turbines and generators and the source of healing in oxygen chambers. Of course, we could not and would not exist without it. The air around us has the natural mystical capacity not only to sustain our bodies but also to balance our feelings and align our communication landscape.

The air we breathe is always available to us. But it will come to our rescue only if we call upon it—inhaling and exhaling attentively, through our "knowing" nose. Just as our nose filters and cleanses the air we breathe, attentive breathing carries that further, internally filtering and cleansing our thoughts and feelings.

Yes, we should capitalize on the amazing gifts of this knowing nose and use this sense to nurture deeper connections with our kids. So, parents, don't be afraid to "nosedive" into a situation. If you smell trouble, don't bypass it. Step in. It's okay to be "nosy" if it's in your children's best interest. Most of all, remember to add five deep breaths to your go-to tools!

Taste — the Power of Words

The movement of our tongue against the roof of our mouth, our teeth, and our lips not only helps us eat and drink effectively; it also helps us shape our sounds into words. Like our other sense organs, the tongue has multiple functions. Isn't it natural, then, for the taste buds on our tongue to not only identify the flavors of the food we eat but also contribute to the "taste" of our words? Don't the words we use have "flavor" too? Of course they do. That is why phrases like *bitter sarcasm* and *whispering sweet nothings* and *He has an acid tongue* are common. We often use *spicy language* to mean something is risqué or *salty humor* to signify profanity. And haven't you said or heard that some situation has left a *bad taste* in one's mouth?

What rolls off our tongues—our voice and the words we utter—is integral to our communication skills. Yet too often there is a gap between what we *want* to say and what we end up saying.

My natural response when my children messed up unacceptably was, "What were you thinking?" Looking back, I can see that my tone of voice and facial expressions pretty much conveyed the heart-breaking message *Are you stupid?* And of course, whatever the kids had done wrong, the fact is that they weren't really thinking it through or they weren't thinking at all. After all, they are kids—and we all know that being impulsive is very much part of being a child.

As the kids got older, my daughter's response to "What were you thinking?" was always, "I'm so sorry." Then, to make sure she was getting the point, I would respond, "Sorry about what?"

"To whatever it is that you're mad about," she would say.

And that would infuriate me. My comeback—"And you don't know what 'whatever' is?"—would invariably result in her tears. So then I had to deal with the tears, too! Sometimes I even forgot where we'd started and why I was yelling, because my words had taken us far off track.

My son always responded to "What were you thinking?" by crossing his arms, lowering his eyes, and pouting. "I don't know," he'd say.

I would push for an answer. "What do you mean 'I don't know'?"

"I don't know," he'd say again.

I only got angrier; my eyes dilated, my nostrils flared.

"It means, 'I don't remember,' Mom." By now Navin's body language was mimicking mine—dilated eyes, flared nostrils. "I already answered your question five times."

"Don't be disrespectful," I'd snap back. Within moments I'd gotten totally off track again, and I'd taken him with me.

Then I stumbled on the life-transforming work of Yvonne Oswald—therapist and author of the best-selling *Every Word Has Power: Switch on Your Language and Turn on Your Life*. She opened my eyes to an awareness of my thoughts and "self-talk," and I came to realize how my language affected my life. As I became more and more aware of the power of words, I started to take note of my own use of language—how the things I said to my kids affected their feelings and reactions. Soon I started to chuckle at the senseless questions I had been asking them—*What were you thinking? What's wrong with you?* and *How dare you speak to me like that?* None of those questions had a rational answer, and all were coated with fear, quite opposite from my underlying intention of love. The words always left me feeling bad, doubtful, and full of guilt. Now I knew why. As Dr. Oswald says,

"[Our words] not only describe our world but actually create it."[15] They can either keep us on track or take us off of it.

We are constantly teaching our kids the social and emotional skills they need to succeed in their environments—what words to use when they speak to their teachers, friends, and family members. There is no need to work so hard to teach them, however, if we exemplify this ourselves. If our words and tone of voice are respectful and don't hurt others' feelings—our children's, first and foremost—then our children won't know any other way of speaking.

"That's scary," said a mom in a class, sounding concerned. "Am I going to have to learn how to speak 'properly'? I'm exhausted just thinking about it."

Here's what has worked for me and for many other parents: Pick the favorite term of endearment that you use when speaking lovingly to your child—*darling, honey*, whatever—and use it even when you are angry. My pet words for my kids are *love, babloo* ("dear" in Hindi), and *jaan* ("my life" in Hindi). Even when I am angry, I try to remember to use one of these terms right away. It took a while to completely switch from *What were you thinking?* to *What were you thinking, love?* But I was amazed to find that it had a profound effect on my tone of voice! The very taste of the word *love* or *dear* actually made my tone of voice more loving and compassionate, even though I was angry. The addition of one word and the shift in tone produced a totally different response from my kids: "I'm so sorry. I can't believe I even did that or said that."

Our words can either drive our kids to close up and be defensive or encourage them to open up and drop their guard. The more we use terms of endearment in place of words of "enfearment," the kinder we sound and the easier it becomes to communicate with our kids.

Words of endearment tone down the volume of emotions and engage the intellect. Don't get me wrong; do follow through with the appropriate discipline or grounding. But remember to use words that match the intention of the larger goal: your loving relationship with your kids. If adding that one term of endearment can change the outcome of a single conversation, imagine the powerful changes it can bring over the course of childhood years. When you're talking to your kids, sprinkle your words with love so they taste good to both you and your child.

For me, another calming trigger is an affirmation I wrote, inspired by quotes from Anne Lamott[16] and Dr. Wayne Dyer[17]: *When I am right, I will practice being kind, first.* Ever notice how commanding or sarcastic our words and tone of voice get when we know we are right? And with our kids, let's face it, we are right a lot. Naturally, then, we are commanding and sarcastic a lot more than we should be.

I remember one day, lying with my five-year-old daughter on the grass, when she asked, "Mama, why do we have to follow rules?"

"Because rules help us be a better person. They teach us how to behave better," I answered.

"Do mommies and daddies have to follow rules?" she asked.

"Of course they do," I reassured her.

"I know you make *my* rules. Who makes *your* rules, Mommy?"

I instinctively answered, "God does."

Nitasha paused. "How come God doesn't make my rules?" she asked with a frown.

"Because parents make the rules for little kids." I was wondering where she was going with this. "Would you like it better if God made your rules?"

"Yeah, I think so."

"Why?"

"Because Grandma says God talks in a silent voice that we can still hear. And when *you* talk about rules, you always say them loud and not nicely!"

I decided to poke a bit. "Like how?"

"Like when you say, 'How many times have I told you to pick up your toys after you're done playing?'" she imitated me.

She was right. I did do that.

What I didn't learn from my studies of personal growth, my kids taught me! As I watched my words and tone of voice more carefully, I saw that more than half of what I actually wanted to say was not what I ended up saying. Busy-ness and emotions got in the way. There's no way to avoid those things. The life of almost every parent is packed with millions of things to do and tons of emotions to feel. But taking even a couple of deep breaths slows down this loaded momentum. It can activate our PGS and remind us to use terms of endearment; it can help remind us of the affirmation that it's most important to be kind when we are right. It buys us time to transform an impulsive reaction to a thought-out response—and helps keep unpleasant, hurtful words from rolling off the tip of our tongue.

There's also the other time-tested and accessible resource that I mentioned earlier, which can help us do the same.

The Water We Drink

Seventy percent of the human body is made up of water. Water not only hydrates us from the inside but also cleanses our bodies on the outside. Water is an excellent absorber of heat, which is why it serves as a coolant in machinery. Yes, the water we drink, like the air we breathe, also has infinite potential in managing our inner communication landscape: Drinking water hydrates a dry situation. Water can minimize and even absorb the heat of our emotions. Put simply, it cools us down.

Anger and emotional upsets draw a lot of water from our system, which is why our mouth ends up feeling "dry" during an argument. Drinking water brings our body back into balance—into a flow, if you will.

I've experimented with water extensively, and it has proved to be quite the cooling companion in many a heated situation. Every time there is a need for a serious discussion, I always start by pouring two glasses of water—one for myself and one for the child in question. I take sips every few minutes throughout the discussion and, watching me, so does my son or daughter. I've been amazed at how this has helped me to stay cool and prevented me from "blowing a fuse"— uttering the many detrimental words that were rattling around in my head. A few quick chugs of water also helps me cleanse my palate and choose tasteful words, the ones in sync with what I truly wanted to say! Drinking water slows down the momentum of my racing thoughts and emotions.

And as I stay cool and choose my words well, my kids match their responses to mine. Author James Baldwin once said, "Children have never been very good at listening to their elders, but they have never failed to imitate them." Yes, they will do as we do and not as we say.

Verbal Hygiene

Another communication and health habit—"verbal hygiene"—may be a tough one for some young parents to adopt. I recall a scene from years ago, when a next-door neighbor—the F-bomb queen— and I were chatting outside while our sons were playing. When her four-year-old son used the F-word, she screamed, "How many times have I told you not to say that?" She very obviously pretended to be surprised that her child had cursed, but honestly, I was not surprised at all. To make it worse, she followed it up with: "He is learning all kinds of crazy words since he started going to school."

He didn't need school to teach him that word. His mother had taught him well. Children are sponges. They soak it all up—the good, the bad, and the ugly.

In our house, especially as the kids were growing up, foul language was always unacceptable. Every now and then my husband would slip, and I'd respond with, "Absolutely unacceptable!" At first he would respond, "Honey, you didn't grow up here. It's just another common word that expresses anger." Now he knows better than to use that as an excuse!

As I was telling this story in one of my classes, a new mom added, "Lucky you. My husband even uses the word to express how happy he is. I guess it's okay now, since our daughter is only nine months old, and he says he'll stop as soon as she starts talking. I can't really *stop* him—he's an adult!—but I keep checking him on it. I don't know what to do. It's such a habit for him."

It's not easy to change a habit, but we're definitely more motivated to try when we know it has negative effects in the long run. Why do we put so much emphasis on good habits of oral hygiene, for example? We do so because we know the repercussions: bad teeth, gingivitis, plaque. Isn't it easier to cultivate good habits now, than to pay for bad habits later? Similarly, implementing and maintaining good verbal hygiene habits now will be a lot less painful for everyone later.

"But don't kids end up being exposed to those words as they get older anyway?" asked another mom.

Sure they do! My sixteen-year-old son was watching football with a potty-mouth friend who "accidentally" cursed three times in our presence in an hour. I finally told him that I would really appreciate it if he watched his language while in our home. Did that make him stop cursing permanently? Probably not. Did he ever curse in our presence again? Never. As they stretch and squeeze themselves into maturity, kids are going to push the boundaries—that's their job. And, for their own benefit, kids need to be reminded of boundaries—that's *our* job.

Later that evening my son, obviously upset, said, "Mom, that wasn't cool. You're not his mom, and I don't think it was your place to scold him like that. I was embarrassed. It's not like I don't know every curse word in the world." He went on, "You don't have to worry about me being exposed to them anymore. It's not like we have any little kids around. And honestly, even *I* curse sometimes. Everyone does."

I looked my son right in the eye and sat down to explain my thinking. "Navin, first of all," I said, "he was in our house, and it is our job to set the standards. Secondly, I know you know all about curse words. I also know you know all about sex. Does knowing about sex make it okay for parents to start watching porn with their kids?"

Flabbergasted by the analogy, Navin's reaction was, "That's so out of line, Mom. I can't believe you even said that. That's so inappropriate!"

"That's exactly my point, Navin," I said calmly. "You and your friends might know all the curse words in the world, but you also have to know what's appropriate and what's not. As for you cursing, it's your choice. If you make a habit of cursing, you will pass it on to your kids. If you want your kids to curse at you, that's your choice. However, since I don't want mine to, I'll maintain these standards in my house. I hope I've made myself clear."

That night, at the dinner table, Navin admitted that he saw my point about setting the standards at home and added that he wouldn't want his own kids to curse either.

When we are bold enough to take a stance and explain it so they can relate instead of blowing a fuse or being unkind, our kids will get the picture. If we want respectful kids who don't curse, then we have to be respectful and practice not cursing ourselves. And if you have a partner or spouse who does use profanity around the kids, it is your job to voice your disagreement. Only with determination and conviction can you align your end goal with your daily actions.

Rudyard Kipling was right when he said that words are "the most powerful drug used by mankind." Words can both heal and hurt; they can fill our hearts with joy or sadness. Words can make or break a situation. Words can also help us bend, mend, and transcend the outcome of any situation. They reform and transform.

And if it's a habit, try holding bad words so they never go beyond your tongue: Sometimes when I'm really mad and can sense something not so tasteful building up in my mouth, I roll up the tip of my tongue against the roof of my mouth to prevent the words from slipping out. Remind yourself that tasteful words will help you bypass negative emotions—yours *and* your children's. And if you don't choose your words well, your negative language will mask your positive intentions, no matter how good those intentions are.

To our children, words are messages that we imprint on their clean, blank slates. Through words and behavior, we shape and mold our children and their future. Developmental biologist Dr. Bruce Lipton, in his research-packed book about relationships, *The Honeymoon Effect,* notes that children not only listen to their parents but also carefully "mimic their behavior by downloading it into their subconscious minds."[18] When parents exhibit good behavior, that can improve a child's ability to learn the skills for success in this world; when parental behavior is less than stellar, it can drag the child's life "into the ground."

Is all this a huge responsibility for parents? Or as the mom mentioned earlier asked, "Will I have to learn to speak 'properly'?" No, being mindful about your speech is not something unfamiliar or elaborate that you'll have to learn. It's not a new language. It's simply a new attitude, a fresh perspective. Using respectful and kind words is not alien to any of us. We know how to do it. We don't have to learn to speak properly, just appropriately.

"Do you curse and speak disrespectfully to your child's teachers or principal?" I asked the mom.

"Oh no," she said. "That's when I'm at my best behavior."

"Why?" I asked her.

"Because I want to maintain a pleasant and respectful relationship—and I don't want my kid kicked out of school, obviously," she responded.

Well, that's the same reason we need to use our "best behavior"—both attitude and words—with our children: so they don't kick us out of their life, and we don't rob ourselves of the pleasures that parenting should bring us.

Just remember to pause by taking a few deep breaths or a chug of water, and you will do the job with the finesse of the finest writer and the patience of the finest teacher. I truly believe that a mindful choice of words precedes all else in strengthening our connection with our kids and in harnessing their inner perfection—their self-confidence, self-respect, self-esteem, self-worth, and most of all, self-love.

Remind yourself often of the hidden power in words: Distasteful words drown us in doubt, guilt, and fear, whereas tasteful words free us of those same heavy emotions. Commit to watching your words for just one week. You will notice a tremendous difference in how much more confident and fulfilled you feel as a parent. The response you get from your kids will be your big incentive for making kindness a lifelong communication habit.

Touch — the Magic of Contact

When the topic of touch was brought up during one of my parenting classes, a friend and fellow mom—who is also an RN and the director of a neonatal intensive care unit—brought up some amazing examples of the power of touch from her experience working with premature babies for more than fifteen years. She later invited me to tour her unit, where many of the high-risk premature births are drug related. Since drug-dependent mothers are often reluctant to accept the responsibility of their children, let alone bond with them, the nurses nurture these premature babies as best that they can to help them catch up with the natural development that is their birthright.

"One of the most effective methods that helps our babies and their parents bond," said my friend, "is what we call 'skin to skin.'" She continued:

> Our unit advocates and implements the "golden hour," a program in which parents and child share skin-to-skin contact in the first hour after birth. The golden hour helps with attachment and bonding, increases the success rate of breastfeeding, and enhances the baby's immune system. It aids thermoregulation, glucose stability, and the transition to life outside the womb. Babies who experience "skin to skin" also generally have more stable vital signs and demonstrate improved bonding. We see it every day. It all begins with a physical touch that clearly improves the well-being of the baby.

I left the neonatal unit with a new respect and awe for the nurses who step in to help these newborn babies who otherwise would have missed out on receiving the priceless benefits of personal touch at this pivotal moment. As I walked away, I remembered the words of our temple's spiritual leader, who once said, "Each one of us is a source of *prana* (life energy) in each other's lives. By way of a touch, a listening ear, or a soft tone of voice, life force energy can be infused very simply. All it takes is intentional acts of kindness, compassion, and empathy. That is God-likeness. It's nothing outside of us. It's all very much within each one of us." That's exactly what these nurses are doing. Through intentional kindness, compassion, and empathy, they are actually infusing life energy into new life.

Think about it: The very *first* thing that infuses this life energy into newborns is touch. Michelangelo knew that even in the sixteenth century, when he said, "To touch is to give life." Like Michelangelo, we parents are the poets, architects, sculptors, and painters of our children's lives. And we do it all through a love whose very first connection is nurtured most strongly through touch.

This holds true not just for newborns, by the way, but also for children in the womb. Science has shown that pregnant women who touch and caress their bellies soothe not only themselves but also the growing baby, fully delivering the message of love in a single touch from mother to child. A true miracle of nature!

What's even more miraculous is that a single touch is felt all over our bodies, through our skin, which is our largest sense organ. Remember the touch of your first love, which sent a tingle through your entire body? Yes, touch is a form of ultra-sophisticated communication. A soft touch can say *I love you* just as clearly as a stronger touch can say *I'm angry at you*. This is why, when our children act out in public, we might first try to calm the situation with a gentle squeeze on the arm that delivers the message *Watch it*.

Science also confirms (as neonatal nurses like my friend know) that touch is a thermoregulator. Not only can it help us gauge the type and temperature of an emotion, but it can help us manage it. Why is it, then, that parents don't intentionally harness the communication potential of touch to regulate and calm emotions during a conflict? I think it's because we have become accustomed to consciously using touch only alongside an expression of love.

When we are happy with our children, we pat them on the back or hug them, conveying, *I am proud of you. I love you.* On the flip side, when children have an emotional meltdown and are crying, parents will hug kids to console them, sending the message *I'm here for you. I love you.* But generally we forget the gesture when we get angry, though, of course, we don't love our kids any less.

When Navin was young and I got upset at him, he would always ask, after the dust had settled, "Do you still love me?" I would always say, "Of course I do," to which he'd reply, "Can you hug me, then?" Although this should have been a signal, I did not yet realize that the sense of touch was so crucial to him.

I only found that out after I took him to an Ayurvedic practitioner because of some allergic reactions. The practitioner found the source of the allergies, but he also told me, "Navin's physical personality is most responsive to touch. Make sure you use that to your and his benefit."

"How so?" I asked, a little confused.

"When he is upset, touch will calm him. When you are upset, he will touch you to calm you. To him, touch reassures him of love. When you have an issue at hand, always touch him while speaking to him, even if it is simply a hand on his shoulder or back."

What a valuable piece of information that was! I put his suggestion into practice, not just to encourage Navin and console him but, at times, also to get through to him about a problem. It has worked every time. Years later, I read *The Five Love Languages of Children*, by Dr. Gary Chapman and Dr. Ross Campbell, and was reassured that "touch" is truly Navin's primary love language.

The important role that touch plays in our lives has become the focus for renowned psychology professor and researcher Dacher Keltner, PhD. Keltner, who wrote the bestseller *Born to Be Good*, is also the cofounder of the Greater Good Science Center at The University of California, Berkeley, which sponsors groundbreaking scientific research into social and emotional well-being. In Keltner's words, "Touch is the *real* action of compassion. It is an unbelievable mechanism of social well-being, and it may very well be the greatest." He concludes that touch enhances compassion, builds communication and relationships, signals safety and trust, calms cardiovascular stress, and promotes cooperation.[19]

The truth is that parents already innately know the feel-good message that our compassionate touch carries to our children. We have known that from the very first time we held our children in our arms. It is why, in times of celebration, we hug our kids in joy; it's why, in times of sadness and melancholy, holding them makes both parent and child feel better. Now you can remind yourself to also use touch to encourage communication generally.

During discussions with your children, rubbing their back, stroking their hair, and lovingly touching their arm makes them feel safe; it lets them know that you love them even though you're upset with them. A simple touch, as Keltner says, supports safety and security and ushers in trust and compassion.

"My four-year-old likes to hold my hand while I'm scolding him," said a mom in my class. That's because the magic of a touch banishes doubt and fear from a child's mind. As for hugs, they speak for themselves. We all know how good they feel for both parents and children. As cartoonist Bil Keane said, "A hug is like a boomerang—you get it back right away."

• • •

By synchronizing our senses, we deepen our connection to the inner landscape of our impressionable children—their feelings and their thoughts. By simply seeing what their eyes are saying, listening to what their heart is feeling, taking deep breaths through our knowing nose, and using tasteful words and our magical touch, we can positively contribute to their inner well-being.

Working together, our five senses act as clear interpreters of the underlying love that we all feel for our children. These senses enable us to bring that love to the forefront, calming our kids' emotions, easing their doubts and fears, and clearly saying to them, in more ways than one, *I love you,* before we say anything else. When we are sense-able parents, we deliver the compassion and trust that make our kids feel safe, secure, and genuinely, unconditionally loved. We encourage them to be happy, think positive, and do good, all the while enhancing communication and strengthening our relationship.

Sensible Parenting, by calming emotions, opens the minds and hearts of both parent and child, preparing them to reason and make sense of every situation together. In that way we unite our senses with those of our children, placing us in the perfect position not only to be reasonable and responsible ourselves—as we'll see in the next chapter—but also to inspire our children to be the same.

 Affirmation Reminder

I am a Sensible and nurturing parent. I use my five senses to see beyond the obvious, be attentive to my child's inner needs, and deliver the love that I feel.

Quick Takeaways

- Make "sense" of an emotional situation by using your senses.

- Make eye contact to let your children see and feel that you acknowledge and understand their point of view.

- Listen mindfully and patiently to connect deeply. Let children complete their thoughts and sentences before offering suggestions, especially when you know they are wrong. And when you are right, practice being kind first.

- Smell situations and be perceptive before responding.

- Practice verbal hygiene to inspire respect from children. Use words that taste good to you and your child, and sprinkle in words of endearment. Then no matter what you are saying, it will be received positively.

- Touch their hearts by using your magical touch to communicate with children.

- Take five deep breaths and sips of water to activate your senses and your PGS when you're challenged. This will buy some time to help calm your emotions, bring clarity to your thoughts, and turn a reaction into a well-thought-out response.

Reasonable and Responsible Parenting:
Branching Out through Understanding

All our knowledge begins with the senses, proceeds then to the understanding, and ends with reason. There is nothing higher than reason.

—*Immanuel Kant*

My parents were great communicators. While my mother sometimes got caught up in emotion, my father was always, always, the sounding board, the "voice of reason." He had the unique gift of bringing harmony to the most chaotic feelings simply by leading in a genuine, calm tone of voice. "I am so sorry if I'm not understanding you," he'd say, "or if you're not understanding me. But there's no reason in this world that should prevent us from talking about it respectfully. You go first, and I'll listen." My reasonable father inspired my siblings and me to talk about and reason through issues, all the while keeping a close watch to see that none of us crossed his well-defined boundaries of respect. In the midst of many heated talks, he would lower the temperature by saying, "Calm and kind, please"—reminding us to maintain a calm tone of voice and to use kind words.

I remember feeling absolutely furious about some issue, and my father's words would immediately make me less defensive. I even remember, during my teen years, being really mad at myself for allowing the issue to resolve so soon; I was mad that I wasn't mad anymore. "How did I let go of that feeling so fast?" I remember thinking. "I know I was right! I should have stayed mad longer."

As a family, we enjoyed quick recovery time, bouncing back with relative ease from this issue and that. Little did I realize then the magnitude of the gift my parents were giving me—the gift of communication. We could talk about anything and everything. Well . . . almost.

Being brought up in a conservative Middle Eastern country with a strong Indian culture at home, the topic of boys was never up for discussion. The upper-school campus of The Indian School, Kuwait—the academic institution I attended—had two shifts: all girls in the morning from 7 a.m. to 1:30 p.m. and all boys from 2 p.m. to the end of the day. The extent of my interaction with boys was the glance-and-giggle exchanges outside of the school at the shift change, when all the boys showed up before the final bell of the girls' shift. Besides that, in my teen years, I was allowed to interact with boys only at family or friends' get-togethers and dinners, where parents were always present. The few times I was busted by my mom for talking to a boy on the phone or behind the school bus outside of school (where my mom made random, unannounced pickups because she just "happened to be in the area"), we got into heated arguments.

"What's wrong with talking to boys?" I would say, defending myself.

"Good girls from respectable families don't do that. You'll understand when you grow up," my mom would answer.

"What does that even mean, Mom? Just because I talked to a boy does not make me a 'bad' girl," I'd scream back, hurt and offended by her comment.

"You'll understand when you grow up and have children of your own," my mom would say to my fourteen-year-old self.

"Why don't you *get* it, Mom?" I said to her once. "That's such an old-fashioned attitude. If Grandma said that, I'd understand. She's much older. But not you! We live in the seventies, not in the fifties. There's nothing wrong with talking to boys. You have to trust me!" I struggled to make her see my point of view.

Though my parents and I could come to an agreeable understanding of one another's point of view on just about anything else, on this topic we were divided. Once I even tried to reel my dad into a conversation about the subject, and he said, "It's not you we don't trust; it's the world around you. Talk more to your mom about this, my child." And he walked away. In those days, in Indian households, dads and daughters simply did not discuss boys. As for moms, it seemed they didn't mind opening up a conversation, but only to gather information on their daughter's mind-set in order to shut down discussion with an unreasonable, "I don't have to give you a reason for everything. *No means no.*" After trying a couple of times to get through to them, I finally gave up.

Did that stop me (or my many friends in similar situations) from talking to boys or having boyfriends? On the contrary! Those of us who were "restricted" sneaked around and defied the system all the more.

Did we ever get caught? Many, many, many times. By the time I was sixteen, it had become a game. We girls went behind our parents' backs to do what we were not allowed to do, and our moms played detective—sniffing around, looking for clues, and busting us now and then. We didn't get their *No means no* attitude, and they couldn't get through to us because of it.

Fast-forward some thirty years. A family friend approached me to seek my opinion on an issue with her daughter. "I have tried everything," she told me, sounding confused, angry, and hurt all at the same time. She declared:

> Everything in the world is more important to her than her schoolwork. She just doesn't care. And I can't get through to her. What's wrong with her? Or maybe it's me! I'm so worried . . .
>
> It starts with school issues, and then it snowballs. I feel awful about how we just fire back and forth, arguing about everything. She makes me so mad that I start saying the wrong things to her, and I end up feeling guilty afterward. Honestly, I'm scared that she won't graduate. I feel like I'm losing her. I'm even having trouble sleeping.

My friend asked me to speak to her daughter, and I was lucky that the teenager in question agreed to talk with me. I started by thanking her for putting her trust in me. Then I used my dad's oh-so-effective line, which had worked very well with my own children through their teenage years: "I am so sorry that you and your mom are having trouble understanding each other on this issue. But there's no reason in the world that this should prevent us from talking about it respectfully. I'm here for you. You go first, and I'll listen."

The young girl didn't hesitate:

> I don't know what's wrong with my mom. She's my mom, but she just doesn't get me. She says she can't get through to me, but that's because she doesn't ever hear me out. She never listens, and when she does, she's unreasonable. She just blows a fuse every time.
>
> High school has been really hard for me. I'm not like a lot of the other kids with chemistry and algebra. It's just not my thing. So I don't get good grades in those subjects. What's worse is that the chemistry teacher is a friend of my mom. I was dreading being in her class from day one because of that. So my mom gets a weekly progress report from her on this subject. I think my mom is really embarrassed that I'm not doing well in her friend's class, and she feels it makes her look bad. I told her that once, and she yelled back that I'm making an excuse for not trying hard enough.
>
> Plus, this chemistry teacher is such a drama queen. She mocks those of us who aren't doing that great in class, saying, "If you don't get through chemistry, you're not graduating." I hate her!

"Have you told your mom all of this?" I asked.

"I've tried a couple of times, but she doesn't listen," she responded. "She takes it personally, and then we end up arguing. And in the past month we've ended up arguing about everything else, too."

"Why do you think you argue about everything else?" I asked.

The teenager surprised me with the perceptiveness of her answer: "I think it's because I'm angry that she would take the teacher's side instead of her daughter's."

When I asked if she would try discussing this with her mom in my presence, she agreed. I brought three glasses of water from the kitchen and stole a moment alone with her mom. "Reasoning deepens understanding," I explained. "At the very beginning of the conversation, tell her, 'You take the lead.'" The mother agreed, so I went on, "First, when you don't understand something she's saying, instead of getting upset, try to ask her *why*. Second, ask your *whys* calmly and kindly, even if you disagree, or if she says something you don't want to hear. And, third, listen to her until she is done."

When the daughter returned, the mom did just that. Two minutes into the conversation, she calmly and kindly asked her daughter, "Why do you think chemistry is hard for you?"

The girl replied, "I don't *think* chemistry is hard for me; I *know* it is hard for me. There are too many formulas and concepts and too many layers. So much of it has to be memorized, and I have a real hard time with that."

At this point, the child started crying. Her mom held her for a few minutes and then said, "I get it. I'm sorry. I wish I knew that earlier. How about getting a tutor to help?"

"I would love that," replied the girl through her tears, "but the chemistry teacher can't be my tutor. I don't like her."

They both laughed at that. And within a few days, I got a phone call from the mom with an update: They had already found a good tutor, and the past few days had gone well. Not long after, the daughter sent me an email thanking me and joking, "What did you say to my mom?" All of a sudden, they were having longer and calmer conversations about everything. It was not me, of course, who delivered this transformation; it was the power of reasoning with a calm and kind *Why?* Plus the mom's commitment to trying it.

The Calm, Kind Voice of Reason

The answers hidden behind a calm and kind *Why?*—or sometimes a *What?* or a *How?*—open the doors to communication. These simple questioning words have the potential to open the minds of both sender and receiver. When parents ask *Why?* they clearly and directly prompt the child to offer a reason for the behavior. *Reason-able* Parenting, as the word suggests, relies on a parent's ability to reason. Prompting reason, discussion, or logical thinking engages the intellect and helps parents gather and understand information. It takes the fizz out of emotions and prevents emotional spillovers that arguments almost always stir up.

In relationships—particularly between parents and children, where there is a difference in the depth of understanding because of age and life experience—asking *Why?* calmly and kindly helps us build a bridge to understand one another and resolve issues. The energy that parents waste arguing with their children should instead be constructively spent on reasoning and helping kids make sense of the situation. Unreasonable reactions—*Because I said so* and *No means no*—are exhausting and detrimental for both parents and children. Using these familiar phrases taxes your relationship.

This holds true in reverse, too: If you aren't open to answering your child's *Why?*, then you can surely expect him or her to go behind your back, hiding things and serving you disappointment and anguish on a silver platter.

Had I been able to reason with my parents, I know that I would not have hidden so much from them or been so dishonest about boys. If they had answered my *Why?*, perhaps we could have at least reached an acceptable midpoint of understanding. As long as the calm and kind *Why?* is directed toward the *subject* of debate (the issue at hand) and not the *object* of debate (the child), you will be successful at peeling off the layers of emotions and getting closer to an amicable understanding.

After one of my parenting classes, a mom decided to try the calm and kind *Why?* with her academically brilliant thirteen-year-old daughter. When it came to an ongoing argument over dating a boy at school, the mother had always taken the *You're too young* and *No means no* approach. She knew how emotional and sensitive her daughter was, and she strongly felt that the girl was far from ready to date. The next time the topic came up at home, however, the mom took the opportunity to focus on the issue, by calmly and kindly asking, "Why do you think you're ready?" instead of, "Why are you arguing with me?" This approach took the child out of her defensive attitude and onto neutral ground.

"Because I'm a smart girl, Mom," she confidently declared. "I get good grades, and I'm very responsible. I'm smart enough to handle myself."

"I know you are," said her mom. "And I'm very proud of that. But academic intelligence is very different from emotional intelligence. There is a big difference between getting good grades and managing feelings and behavior in a relationship with a boy."

The mom constantly reminded herself to maintain the calm and kind voice of reason; it wasn't difficult, because she saw it was working. And with this very small and easy yet profound communication tool, mother and daughter had a huge breakthrough on the subject. With the communication door now open, they were able to have a good twenty-minute discussion.

The mom honored her daughter by listening to her point of view, which gave her a better understanding of where her daughter was coming from. When the daughter felt that her mom was becoming more approachable about the issue, she admitted that she was a little scared about dating, too. The sensible mother gave her daughter a hug, amazed at how beginning with just one calm and kind *Why?* helped them make so much progress, and led her into Reasonable Parenting!

Yes, it took some personal discipline. As the mom later said in class, she felt vulnerable; she knew that by listening to her daughter, she was opening herself to change, unsure of the outcome of this sensitive subject. But with that first leap of faith, she felt her Parental Guidance System (PGS) fire up, and she saw herself naturally navigating through Honorable, Approachable, and Sensible Parenting.

During the conversation, she calmly walked her daughter through the steps and the responsibility of dating and noticed that her daughter did indeed feel a little scared. In the end, it turned out that her daughter simply wanted to spend some time with a boy who had shown interest in her. She really didn't want to be alone with him just yet. "Can I invite him home on Thursday for our movie night?" she asked. Her mom agreed without hesitation.

When used together, Honorable, Approachable, and Sensible Parenting help us calm the emotions so we can access the intellect. Reasoning then helps us deepen our understanding. Reasoning holds our hand, and takes us from the known to the unknown. It prepares us for change and growth in both the long and short term. Scottish scientist James Dewar is credited with saying, "Our minds are like parachutes; they only function when they are open." How true that is!

Reasoning with a calm and kind *Why?* has the potential to open a child's mind so we, as parents and first teachers, can guide him or her to the next level of growth. Think about the term *raising our children*. We are truly helping them *raise* their level of understanding—of themselves and of the world around them—one experience at a time. When parents commit to being that voice of reason for their children, we help resolve internal doubts. For the teenager having issues with chemistry, for example, reasoning helped by clearing up doubtful thoughts both for the parent (*Will my child make it through high school?*) and for the daughter (*Why doesn't my mom get me?*). Reasoning helps parents "get through" to their children *and* lets children know that their parents are capable of "getting it."

As we know from our communication balance, productive breakthroughs in communication happen when we calm our noisy emotions and allow the intellect to take center stage. A simple *Why?* or *What?* or *How?* can shift the focus from disturbing emotions to productive intellectual engagement—from negative feelings to positive thoughts, from misunderstandings to deeper understanding.

We cannot forget, however, that emotions are very much a part of human nature. We can't and don't want to get rid of them completely. If we did, we would be like robots! I like to think of emotion as *e-motion*, or *energy in motion*. Different e-motions have different effects: Negative e-motion can rev things up and kick a situation into high gear, beyond acceptable speed limits. These emotions that make us mad, sad, sensitive, angry, and impatient are what I call "breakdown emotions," because they break down a stable mind-set and, with it, communication.

Conversely, there are positive emotions that uplift us toward being loving, kind, compassionate, empathetic, and grateful. I like to call these "breakthrough emotions," because they help us break through challenges, putting us in a calm frame of mind—one that enhances communication. That's not to say that one set is altogether "good" and one "bad," however. Both sets of emotions are necessary, and they enhance our self-understanding—a crucial part of growth.

Just as Sensible Parenting deepens connections and opens the heart by pacifying emotions, Reasonable Parenting helps us branch out further: By engaging the intellect, it increases understanding and opens the mind, which instantly helps us listen, become absorbed, and engage our children in a productive conversation. It prompts dialogue and builds trust and self-confidence in both parent and child. Moreover, reasoning helps our children understand themselves and their own emotions, which is a great booster shot for their emotional intelligence, propelling their self-worth and self-esteem.

Understanding also takes both parent and child to the deeper intellectual realm of awareness, reflection, and realization. By being reasonable, parents are encouraging and developing "mindsight," which we discussed in the chapter on Honorable Parenting. As psychiatrist Dr. Daniel Siegel reminds us, "Mindsight is our human capacity to perceive the mind of the self and others. It is a powerful lens through which we can understand our inner lives with more clarity, integrate the brain, and enhance our relationships with others."[20]

Echoing his point, researchers at a group of leading universities have concluded that "Parents' ability to regulate themselves and to remain firm [and] confident and [to] not overreact is a key way they can help their children to modify their behavior. You set the example as a parent in your own emotions and reactions."[21]

Our emotional reactions (and sometimes overreactions) are detrimental to the healthy development of our children. I know many parents whose first instinctual reaction is emotional. We all also know of children who remain supercharged by emotions even at an age when they should be able to manage their day-to-day issues with some composure. That is human nature; we are all wired differently. But science has shown us that, thanks to new research on neuroplasticity, with a little practice we can actually retrain our brains and exercise our capacity to expand and learn new behaviors at any age. So if you're not practicing reasoning already, open up to it—know that you can do it. With a little practice, reasoning will become second nature to you and your children. If, however, parents ignore the opportunity to be reasonable, their children will end up doing the same—and will spend a lifetime mismanaging emotions and missing out on the beauty and depth that parent-child relationships bring to our hearts.

It's simple: Reasonable parents raise reasonable children. The efforts we put into parenting during our children's formative years will result in their healthy development and growth. We have no control over the trials that our children will face, of course, but we can definitely teach them to manage their responses to these challenges. Moreover, when parents make reasoning a family communication habit, it directly supplements a child's academic ability to think critically and solve problems.

And there's a difference between reasoning and arguing: Reasoning is the exchange of thoughts; arguing is the exchange of emotions. Reasoning appeals to a child's intelligence and creates an open forum for discussion. In the absence of reasoning, however, emotions take the lead. In that case neither parent nor child is in charge, and the end result is unnecessary arguments.

As children get older and their brains develop, Dealing with the Feeling can definitely help untangle emotions. But reasoning and the understanding that stems from it will actually help *dissolve* emotions. How? Reasoning or discussions between two minds helps the intellect put the situation in perspective. Then we are better equipped to manage and resolve emotional conflicts and differences in opinion. That's a true platform for growth.

When my son was about fourteen, he called me from his school bus and said, "Mom, you're going to love this 'thought of the day' that I just read on a church sign." (My kids know I love learning from quotes.) This is what he read: *Life is 10 percent what happens to you and 90 percent how you react to it.* That's so true. Situations and issues are only a small part of the equation of life; the larger part is how we react to them and the time and effort we spend trying to clean up emotional debris.

When emotions are heating up, reasoning helps parents manage their expressions and responses—their actions and behavior—and that is what leaves lasting impressions in our children's minds, sometimes for a lifetime. It is these very expressions that define responsible—or response-able—parenting.

Being Response-able

I promise that if you take a leap of faith with your kids by *reasoning* about a repetitively challenging situation, you will make progress by *responding* instead of *reacting*. A response is simply a well-thought-out reaction—one that involves engaging your own and your child's intellect.

Most of the time, we don't have to think about either reacting or responding. Despite the endless tasks involved, family life is fun—fulfilling and soul satisfying.

As long as our children are following our lead and doing what they're "supposed" to do, love is in the air, and all is peaceful on the home front. But what happens when children decide to test the waters? What happens when they talk or behave in an "unacceptable" manner? All hell breaks loose! This is when our habits of reacting or responding come to the fore.

To bring this point alive, here's an example that I share in all my classes when this topic is addressed: A teenager has an issue at school. He walks through the front door of his home, flings his backpack on the floor, and heads for his room, slamming his bedroom door. An alarmed parent follows him upstairs and from the other side of the locked door says, "Excuse me, young man. This is unacceptable behavior. What's your problem?"

"It's none of your business," answers the boy disrespectfully. "I don't want to talk about it."

"As long as you're in my house, it's my business," exclaims the parent. "Don't you dare talk to me like that!"

"You're mean. Leave me alone," barks back the teenager.

"That's it! You're grounded!" shouts the parent. "I'm sick and tired of your behavior! You're not going to Zack's party this weekend."

In this reactive household, the teenager is grounded before the parent even knows what the real issue is. The boy ends up directing his anger toward the parent, prompting a reaction from the parent as well. Their unrecognized, uncontrolled emotions hinder communication and get in the way of solving the problem—which gets in the way of their relationship.

Now, let's play out the same situation in a response-able household, where parents and kids have developed and learned to trust the habit of talking things out—where being reason-able and response-able is a family communication habit. Same initial action: A teenager has an issue at school. He walks in the front door, flings his backpack on the floor, and heads straight to his room, saying, "I'm so pissed at Jeffrey. I'm going upstairs." He's gotten used to putting his emotions into words and mentioning the reason for his anger, so his actions make sense to the parent, who feels justified leaving the boy alone until he is a little less emotional.

The teenager feels confident that he'll get the space he needs, so he doesn't close or lock his bedroom door. After allowing a brief cooling-off period, the parent knows it's possible to approach the boy to help out. In this case, the parent rubs the son's back and asks, "Why are you angry at Jeffrey, buddy?"

Out comes the story: "I'm so done with Jeffrey!" the teen says. "He claims to be my best friend, but I saw him talking to Melissa and asking her out when he knows darn well that I have a crush on her, and I've been trying to find a way to ask her out. I know she likes him, too, but he should have backed off! He's more interested in Sonia anyway—and he *knows* that I like Melissa. What a jerk!"

With those details prompted by a calm and kind *Why?* the parent could help the son figure out how to *respond* to his friend. This sort of exchange, especially during turmoil, is what makes both parent and child reason-able and response-able!

As parents, we set the standards. We are the leaders, the teachers, the voices of reason. It is up to us to navigate the way to harmony, so our children can follow. Children are not wired to *respond intellectually*—they are wired to *react emotionally.* As they grow and develop, it becomes our job to rewire them and teach them by example.

After all, kids might be smart, but even in our children's teenage years, only 80 percent of their brains are developed. Sometimes they can't get their emotions out of the way to make sense of a situation. As an article in *Harvard* magazine noted: "Research . . . powered by technology such as functional magnetic resonance imaging has revealed that young brains have both fast-growing synapses and sections that remain unconnected. This leaves teens easily influenced by their environment and more prone to impulsive behavior, even without the impact of souped-up hormones and any genetic or family predispositions."[22] As young brains mature, these synapses make connections based on environmental experiences.

Transitioning from breakdown emotions to breakthrough emotions is one way to help our children connect the synapses and move from reacting to responding. Keep in mind, though, that breakdown emotions like fear and anger are not necessarily bad. They bring clarity to what we *don't* want, which is necessary in order to be clear about what we *do* want. Breakdown emotions might seem dark, but that's just because they're waiting for us to shine some light on them. And as we do, they start to fade and then disappear. Anger can be brightened at any time with love and patience, and sadness can be lightened by kindness and understanding.

As adults, we bear the burdens of the world on our shoulders. Even when we become honorable, approachable, sensible, and reasonable and responsible parents, we are still merely human beings. We are bound to have our own breakdowns, and that's okay. But when we do, how we recover from them is paramount.

Reflect, Redirect, Reconnect

What happens if, during a disagreement, you were not able to activate your PGS and tune in to being reasonable, and instead you've reacted impulsively? Well, after the storm has passed and the dust has settled, honor your efforts as a parent and tell yourself it's okay to make a mistake. Then take a few minutes to make some mental notes on the residue of emotions. Do you feel bad? Are you feeling guilty? Notice also how your child is feeling. Is he or she angry? Sad? This period of transition is called *reflection*.

As you reflect, you are placing emotions in perspective, and this will automatically start to make you feel calmer. Reflection is pure internal intellectual engagement—a surefire way to turn down the internal emotional temperature. As we discussed in the section on Sensible Parenting, taking five deep, calming breaths and drinking some water is a terrific way to enhance reflection. Bring a glass of water to your child, too, and ask him or her to take a few deep breaths. Appeal to your kids' understanding by telling them, "Water will help us engage our brain and calm our emotions so we can resolve this issue." (My kids rolled their eyes at first, but eventually they got it, and now, as adults, they turn to it themselves.) Be sense-able. Give a hug or pat an arm, and say you'd like to revisit the situation. Then start over: First, apologize for your meltdown. Then, reason and respond.

When we commit to reflect, it helps us *redirect* a situation in the direction of progress, which is growth. Why is a trying issue called a "challenge"? Because it challenges us to evolve and grow. Challenges are invitations for us to use our intellect to understand and redirect our emotions, to make better choices so we can guide ourselves and our children toward breakthrough emotions and communication. During reflection, consider the issue on hand as a "challenge" instead of a "problem." This simple substitution of words helps me shift my attitude. It inspires me to "rise to the challenge" and redirects my internal perspective toward a resolution. Then, by example, we can intelligently raise our children's level of understanding as well.

As for our kids, they are both resilient and forgiving. They are waiting to be heard. They want to communicate as much as we do. They want to be loved just as much as we want to love them. They want us to show them and tell them how much we love them. And only parents can give them what they need, wholeheartedly and unconditionally. Always remember that actions speak as loud as words do. When our actions and words are aligned with our intention, it brings communication into balance and we all win. Being a reasonable and response-able parent will help you do just that. It will show your kids the love you feel for them; it will help you *reconnect*, and it will build their self-confidence by teaching them, too, how to be reasonable and responsible.

So if, for whatever reason, you have ended up reacting to a situation, a quick and timely break to *reflect, redirect*, and *reconnect* will put you right back on the path to being able to respond—to being "response-able"—and will reopen the door to communication.

As you develop and encourage this family communication habit, don't be surprised if your children start to reason with you, too. And when they do, listen to them open-mindedly and consider their ideas. Let them take the lead, for they are fully equipped to facilitate our growth just as much as we are equipped to facilitate theirs.

A close friend has two sons, ages ten and seven, who got into a fight over an iPod Touch. The older brother had one. The younger boy did not; his parents had told him he had to wait until he was older. One day, he slipped his older brother's iPod into his pocket and hid in the other room so he could play with it. When he got caught, he slammed the device on the floor, and his brother reacted by pushing him.

When the screaming started, the mom moved in and separated the boys. She calmed the older brother by Dealing with the Feeling and agreeing that she would be angry, too, if her little brother had done that. She promised him that she would talk to the younger boy and see what he had to say to justify his behavior.

The younger boy was also angry. "He pushed me!" he cried.

"I understand that," responded his mom. "However, you know you should not have sneaked his iPod away without his permission. Please tell me why you would do that." Her tone was calm and kindly.

"Because he gets to have an iPod, and I don't," the boy reasoned. "Why do I have to wait until I turn nine? Why does he get to have an iPod Touch when I'm more responsible with my things than he is?"

This mom knew her young son had a valid point, and she told him so. She promised that she would speak with his dad and that they would consider his reasonable request. In the meantime, he was to promise he would not take his older brother's iPod without permission. His eyes lit up, and he agreed and even apologized to both his mom and his brother. His birthday arrived two months later; through intelligent reasoning, he had earned his own iPod Touch.

When parents are open to reconsidering a reasonable request, children are encouraged to reason, which helps them build lasting communication habits that will serve them throughout life, in school, in a career, and among family and friends. Now, that is truly the greatest return on investment any parent could wish for.

Open-Ended Questions

When you have reasoned and are ready to respond, complete the task by mindfully using tasteful words, as we discussed in the Sensible Parenting section. Make sure they match your intention. Especially during conflict, load your response with words of reason, starting with your calm and kind *Why?* (or perhaps *What?* or *How?*) and finishing with open-ended questions that prompt thought-out answers from your children. I learned this valuable method of communication through years of experience in sales. Simply put, a closed-ended question is one that prompts a *yes* or *no,* an *I don't know,* or even silence; an open-ended question, on the other hand, requires a little more thought and more than a one-word or curt answer.

While adapting a successful sales method to your parenting language might seem strange at first, if you look closely, the connection will become pretty clear: The foundation of both effective sales and effective parenting is communication. Furthermore, the goal of both is nurturing connections and building relationships.

Let's review some common *reactions* parents have in chaotic situations and reword them as *responses* by incorporating open-ended questions that prompt more than a *yes* or *no* answer. You'll be surprised how changing or adding a few words can make a world of difference in opening up communication.

Reaction		Response
I can't believe you did that!	$\longrightarrow$	Why do you think you did that, love?
What were you thinking?	$\longrightarrow$	What distracted you from making the right decision?
What is wrong with you?	$\longrightarrow$	Why did you think that was appropriate?
How many times have I told you not to do this?	$\longrightarrow$	What did we talk about when we discussed this last time?

Using open-ended sentences after the *Why, What,* or *How* really helps open up the conversation by steering the child away from giving *yes, no,* or other unresponsive answers. Framed in this context, your questions will prompt your child's intellect to participate and help your child reflect on what he or she did, and why. When children reflect, they, too, will be better able to redirect their feelings and behavior. Of course, your calm and kind response also will go a long way toward encouraging a more productive answer from your child.

When I give these examples of closed-ended and open-ended questions in my parenting classes, I can see the frustration in the parents' expressions and hear it in their comments: "This is going to be hard," they say. "I just don't talk like this." Or "I'm going to have to watch my every word. It's going to require some effort, and I already have so much on my plate . . ."

My answer is, yes, it is going to require some effort, but the energy you put in now is so much less than the effort and energy you will need to pick up the pieces if you don't think ahead. It is much easier to instill a new habit than it is to bear the consequences of repeated communication breakdowns. And the younger our kids are, the easier it is to introduce new habits of communication. As children get older, issues get bigger.

If you are already in the habit of reasoning and responding, you might have less work to do in order to restore balance and harmony when your children drift away. In the course of raising kids, both parents and children are going to face many challenges—with friends, family, academic issues, boyfriends and girlfriends, driving safety, alcohol, drugs, teenage pregnancy, to name but a few. This is a fact. But how we reason, respond, talk through, and communicate about these issues is what will define our children's character and lead to a harmonious environment at home.

Times have changed. Our children are part of a generation that is being raised on the information superhighway. Through search engines or social media networks, it seems that the answer to their every question is at their fingertips. They know how space shuttles work and why revolutions happen in other countries. Both on the web and in their academic institutions, they are used to absorbing and understanding information through reasoning. That's really how they learn best. In fact, reasoning is how most of us learn best. Now we parents just have to focus on using our children's already

refined reasoning skills to enhance communication and relationships at home.

Whether you are a parent of a young child or a teenager, being
reasonable and response-able will help you build and strengthen
communication habits. And if you are pregnant or have an infant,
be forward thinking. Start instilling this good communication habit
by practicing it with your spouse, family, and friends. It will benefit
you in the long run with your children—plus, it will strengthen your
communication with your other loved ones, too.

All parents share a common goal of teaching kids to respond to life
thoughtfully instead of simply reacting. Well, that training and guidance has to start with the parents. If making these sorts of changes
seems hard for you, look at it as a challenge to better your family life
and to strengthen your children's self-confidence. As with the other
tools discussed in this book, it is just a matter of committing to balanced communication—in this case, through reasoning and responding. And when you go off track, breathe deeply, hydrate, cool off,
and then take a minute to reflect, redirect, and reconnect. As Peggy
O'Mara, former editor and publisher of *Mothering* magazine, says,
"The way we talk to our children becomes their inner voice." Indeed,
our responses and expressions leave lasting impressions on our children. The importance of these impressions cannot and should not be
underestimated.

Expressions and Impressions

If how we speak to our children becomes their inner voice, surely our
own parents' voice resides within us. As Dr. Shefali Tsabary tells us
in her book *Out of Control*, "The patterns of behavior we witness in
childhood become the template for our own way of parenting." This
is a topic of concern often discussed in my classes by both moms and

dads: "I'm starting to sound like my mom when I speak to my kids!" They share with me their stories of communication struggles with their children, which they believe stem from their communication struggles with their own parents. One mother said she hated it when her father spoke to her a certain way, and yet she now finds herself speaking in exactly the same tone to her children. Another mom said her parents were not very effective communicators, and although she managed to break the cycle, one of her siblings is still in therapy at age forty because of their upbringing.

Poor communication skills and a weak parent-child relationship can be a challenging cycle to break. Other parents have told me, "This is how my parents raised me. I don't know any different. What I do know is that it works for one of my children but not for the other."

These common concerns about emotional legacies and communication struggles between parents and children have been beautifully addressed by Dr. Tina Bryson and Dr. Daniel Siegel in an article from the online publication *This Emotional Life*. They write: "The most important factor when it comes to how you relate with your kids and give them all those advantages, is how well you've made sense of your experiences with your own parents." This is where the *reflect, redirect, and reconnect* philosophy will serve you well. Bryson and Siegel conclude:

> Regardless of your upbringing, and whatever happened to you in your past, you can be the loving, sensitive parent you want to be, and raise kids who are happy, successful, and fully themselves. It all starts with reflecting on your experiences and developing a coherent life narrative. Then you can feel confident that you're ready to create the kind of relationship with your children that promotes

> integration and well-balanced lives. As a result, you
> can all [the] more easily survive the daily challenges,
> and truly thrive.[23]

We all have a past, and sometimes it feels as though we are strug-
gling to escape it. Reflection can help us put our past in perspective and redirect our emotions. When we become aware of the
unhealthy impact of our inherited relationship issues, we can better understand the importance of the change we want to advocate
moving forward in the relationship with our children. Reflection on
our past can help us redirect our buried emotions so that they lose
power over us, breaking the cycle. This is the only way to reconnect
wholly, to solidify strong connections with our kids in the future.
Take that stance and, as Mahatma Gandhi said, "Be the change you
want to see."

And while you're at it, go ahead and forgive your parents. Surely
they did the best job that they could, based on their own abilities, circumstances, and resources—you might find this easier to accept now
that you're a parent yourself. Letting go of painful past feelings helps
free up your inner landscape for more breakthrough emotions such
as compassion and empathy—which you'll need while raising your
own children and for your own health. The late, renowned neurosci-
entist Candace Pert, in her groundbreaking book, *Molecules of Emotion*, points out how emotions affect not only our minds and how we
think, but also our physical bodies and how we feel. Emotions affect
our entire well-being—another solid reason to encourage us to shift
to breakthrough emotions and communication. Breakthrough emotions also invite our intelligence to participate, clearing the way for us
to be both reasonable and response-able.

Yes, our expressions will leave an impression on our children's future communication habits. Hurtful expressions hinder our larger goal of nurturing a lasting relationship with our children, and they leave behind an emotional legacy that is not conducive to raising kids to be happy, think positive, and do good.

On the other hand, the emotional legacy of robust expressions of love and happiness will position your children well to make their mark and make the world a better place. It will definitely fuel them for a lifetime, multiplying and traveling forward through your children to your grandchildren and great-grandchildren as well. That is the type of emotional legacy we can all be proud of leaving behind.

• • •

We've come a long way thus far. With Honorable Parenting and Approachable Parenting, we started to *build* our intrapersonal skills, which we use to understand and manage our own *inner* communication landscape. Then, through Sensible Parenting and Reasonable and Responsible Parenting, we *strengthened* our interpersonal skills, which we use to understand and manage our *outer* communication landscape and our relationships with our children. All the while our focus—for both parent and child—has been on keeping emotions in check and revealing our inner perfection by planting self-confidence, growing trust, nurturing connections, and branching out to boost self-esteem, self-worth, and self-respect, all through love and understanding.

Now it's time to reap the fruits of these communication habits and ensure that you have a fulfilling, sweet parenting experience that is both enjoyable and memorable.

Affirmation Reminder

I am a Reasonable, Responsible, and understanding parent. I am a calm and kind voice of reason who encourages open communication and loving emotional expression.

 Quick Takeaways

- Be the calm and kind voice of reason. A simple *Why? What?* or *How?* can turn an emotional situation into a productive intellectual discussion.

- Respond intelligently instead of reacting emotionally, facilitating a communication balance. Reasoning deepens understanding and bypasses arguments; responses trump reactions.

- If you have reacted impulsively, reflect, redirect, and reconnect to put yourself back on the path to being response-able and open the door to communication. Be willing to apologize—it helps redirect the discussion toward progress.

- Use open-ended questions to start the conversation and to extract answers that go beyond *Yes, No,* and *I don't know.*

- Our expressions become our children's impressions. An emotional legacy of robust expressions of love and happiness is what every parent wants to pass on through our children to future generations.

Enjoyable and Memorable Parenting:
Reaping the Fruits

Each day of our lives we make deposits
in the memory banks of our children.
—*Charles R. Swindoll*

Nitasha was five years old when her aunt had her practicing for an intermission parade of children at the Miss L.A. India Beauty Pageant. Ten children wearing beautiful Indian wedding outfits were to walk across the stage and be asked the following questions by a rising Bollywood star: *What is your name? How old are you? Where do you live? What do you want to be when you grow up?*

Nitasha already knew the answer to that final question—she had told us at age four that she wanted to be a "kids' doctor" when she grew up. She suffered from frequent ear infections, and we spent a considerable amount of time in her pediatrician's office. She loved her doctor, who made so many children "feel better." She was a quick learner, so teaching her the word *pediatrician* for her moment on stage was a breeze. But as a precaution, we rehearsed the pertinent questions a few times.

The pageant was to be held in a hotel in Anaheim, California, about fifty miles from our home, so we decided to make a weekend out of it and head out the day before for a trip to Disneyland. For my then-two-year-old son, it was far from the "Happiest Place on Earth." Goofy, Mickey, Minnie, Pluto, and Donald all scared him. Nitasha, however, enjoyed every single moment.

The next day, during the pageant's intermission, out came the cutest little kids, all dressed up in Bollywood wedding attire. The seven kids before Nitasha all wanted to be engineers, doctors, astronauts, architects, lawyers, and scientists—typical of the professions that their high-achieving Indian parents would have encouraged them to pick. As each child spoke, the general responses from the crowd were synchronized *Wows*, *Ahhs*, and *Smart kids*. Then it was Nitasha's turn. I whispered to my husband, "Thank God, she will be original. No one has said 'pediatrician' so far."

"What is your name?" asked the handsome young actor, Rahul Roy, who was moderating the intermission parade.

"My name is Nitasha Khetarpal, and I'm five years old," my little pediatrician quickly answered.

"You're a smart one," said Rahul. "You already answered the next question!"

Nitasha lifted her microphone and said, "Thank you. My mom and dad and everybody say that, too." She giggled.

"Where are your mom and dad?" he asked. We proud parents waved our hands, and a thousand eyes turned to look at us. "So, smart Nitasha, do you already know the answers to the next questions?" Roy asked.

She nodded *yes*.

"Take it away, genius."

At that, my pediatrician answered proudly, "I live in Los Angeles, and when I grow up, I want to be an ice cream girl at Disneyland!"

To this day, I think I blacked out for a second. Then I turned to look at my husband, who was cracking up and getting high fives from the moms and dads around us. It took me a few minutes to even see anything funny in this.

Throughout the afternoon, at least a hundred people came up to us and said that that was the funniest performance ever. But all the mom of the "ice cream girl at Disneyland" wanted to know was what had changed her five-year-old's lifelong ambition.

On our way home, pretending to be casual, I carefully inched my way into the subject. "Did you have fun, Nitasha?" Of course, she did. "You did such a great job. You were so funny. But what made you change your mind from wanting to be a pediatrician?"

"Well, Mom," she said, "when we were at Disneyland yesterday, I saw the face of the ice cream girl, and she looked soooo happy . . . like me. Then I thought of Dr. N and remembered how she is always nodding her head and thinking a lot. I think she's not happy because she has so many sick kids to worry about. That's why I changed my mind. When I grow up, I want to be happy like the ice cream girl at Disneyland."

All kids want is, first and foremost, to be happy. They came into this world happy, and their vision for their grown-up selves is to remain happy. Isn't that what all of us wanted when we were little? We were all prewired to live happily ever after. So how did we parents end up being so stressed and anxious about "raising happiness," to use sociologist Christine Carter's phrase?

The answer is that we lose sight of what our kids really want. Whether our kids are five or fifteen, being happy and feeling loved is what they desire most. It is also what we desire most as parents, as we've discussed throughout this book. And it is this happiness and love between parent and child that translates to joy in our lives; it is what leads us into enjoying this ride. It is what makes our life more enjoyable. We are going to be doing this most important job of parenting for the rest of our lives; why not make the best of it?

And yes, we are going to be faced with situations that steal the happiness away *temporarily.* Circumstances and situations that make us and our kids unhappy will most definitely occur. There will be times when we feel stretched and challenged by the dilemmas of parenting, which naturally tend to mask its joys.

"I used to be such a happy person when I was a teenager and a young adult," one mom shared with me. "I feel like I used to worry about nothing—I was carefree. Much has changed since then, though. I feel like the presence of my kids has taught me to worry, fear, doubt, and feel guilt. That's what takes the joy out of parenting for me."

Experiencing these turbulent emotions—or "parental emotion commotion," as I like to call it—does tend to sometimes take the joy out of parenting. However, our kids have not "taught" us how to worry, doubt, or feel guilty. We have simply reacted to their presence, their ups and downs, and the long list of to-do's with these stressful emotions. And that stress is detrimental for both parents and children. It affects not just our happiness but also our health and that of our kids for a very long time to come. A recent study by Dr. Marilyn Essex of the University of Wisconsin at Madison shows that the stress levels of mothers and fathers affects their kids' DNA, not only as toddlers but even when they become teenagers.[24]

Parental stress or emotional commotion takes us farther from communication breakthroughs and our goal of maintaining a long-term healthy relationship with our kids. Yet we're the ones who set the family environment. Our attitude and our reactions or responses to the challenges of raising kids can play up or down the happiness that our kids thrive on. The choice is ours.

"But this emotional commotion has steered me away from the constantly happy person that I used to be before I had my kids," said the same mom. "As much as I adore my boys, sometimes I'm just so angry at how they have behaved or how they fight with each other."

Kids will be kids. They are going to fight and push the limits. That's what they are supposed to do. It's how they learn and grow. Didn't we do that to our parents? Didn't we mentally and emotion-ally ambush them sometimes? That's life. We go through the emo-tion commotion because we have expectations. We expect our kids to behave well *all* the time. We expect them to be happy, think positive, and do good *all* the time. But that is *our* shortcoming, not theirs. For their part, our kids expect only love and happiness from us. If we also put love and happiness first, we will be better equipped to handle the challenges they bring.

Whatever our expectations, we should always recognize that our kids are "perfect" just the way they are. They are perfect because they are ours. If they were not perfect for us, then they wouldn't be in our lives. Call it fate, God, destiny, or whatever you like. Look around, and you will notice that parents and children fit together like pieces of a puzzle. There is a place where they connect. Whether you have one child or ten, each will fit you perfectly.

When our kids make mistakes we need to remind ourselves that this, too, is part of the enjoyable ride. They will learn from them, as did we. That will help us bounce back and return to our positive outlook. Clouds of unhappiness come in to teach us something, and when we have mastered their lesson, they move on, revealing clear blue skies once again. The sooner we start to understand and accept this, the sooner we will start to enjoy this lifetime ride.

As my kids often remind me, "YOLO, Mom." *You only live once!* We will only have these children once! Let's enjoy the ride and our kids as best as we can. If we strive to make this ride enjoyable, it will naturally be a memorable journey for us.

"It's hard for me to remember that when I'm stressed or stretched too thin," many parents have told me. Yes, it is. But here's a little secret: Behind all the noise of the emotion commotion—both yours and your children's—you can program soothing mental "background music" that can remind you to quiet the noise every time. And once you know the notes of the melodious music, they are guaranteed to uplift your perspective, dissipate the noise, make you feel better, and relieve the stress.

And once these notes become part of our daily lives, they will add an unmatched element of joy into our lives.

The Musical Notes of Gratitude

I remember the excitement that I felt when both my kids spoke their first word: *mama.* My husband, needless to say, was not so happy, because he had been practicing *papa* with them for a long time. Every time he complained, I reminded him that this was my gift, my reward for giving birth. Eventually, we were happy to hear many words from their little mouths, but two of the most gratifying in particular were *thank you.*

Thank you is one of the first phrases we teach our children, and when they learn to apply it well, it makes every parent laugh and beam with pride. *Thank you* is a verbal delivery of gratitude, which is how we think and feel about something in our hearts. *Thank you* acknowledges appreciation, thoughtfulness, and kindness. And researchers in the field of positive psychology have also proved that expressing gratitude boosts the self-worth, self-esteem, self-confidence, and happiness of both the giver and the receiver. The phrase has a ripple effect!

This concept is illustrated in the beautiful children's book (now a movement) *Have You Filled a Bucket Today?* These simple words, *thank you,* hold the power to fill buckets of happiness for the giver, the receiver, and anyone they come into contact with. And the more you get, the more you give, and vice versa. It's contagious. While receiving gratitude makes one feel happy, expressing that gratitude makes us share that happiness.

Gratitude is also a powerful mood elevator, notes Larry Senn, a pioneer in shaping corporate culture and the award-winning author of *Up the Mood Elevator: Your Guide to Success Without Stress.* Senn puts gratitude at the top of his list of feelings that raise the quality of our lives.

Sometimes when we parents are caught in the midst of day-to-day dilemmas, however, we tend to overlook the blessings of our parental experience. Recently a coworker and childhood friend noticed me fretting and asked me what the matter was. I poured out my heart about a parental dilemma. He heard me out, gave me a hug, and looked into my eyes. "Be blessed to have these issues," he said. "Don't waste your time moping. If this has been on your mind for two days, then that's two wasted days of your life and that of your kids. This issue and many more will pass. We waste way too much time by mulling on things like this for long periods. Our time with our kids is precious and priceless. And you know I know that better than anyone else."

Those words instantly shifted my perspective. While I had spent two days focused on my little problem, I did not think about what this friend and his wife were missing. They had lost their fourteen-year-old son a dozen years ago, and even though they have tried to fill that emptiness by being the best parents they can be to their other kids, foster kids, and now grandkids, they still live with an irreplaceable void. I realized that day how easy it is for us parents to get buried in little issues and lose sight of the larger blessings of parenting. All it took was this one noteworthy signal to change back my perspective to one of gratitude.

Another friend of mine, who has worked for the same company for fifteen years, told me, "I am so grateful for this job because I have learned so much, and there is always room for growth. I have climbed the ladder and have a great compensation package, along with excellent health benefits." It's the same with parenting. We learn so much, and there is always room for growth. We climb the ladder from being parents of babies, to parents of toddlers, then preschoolers, high schoolers, young adults, and eventually, many of us end up as grandparents. The compensation package can't be beat: a lifetime of love, joy, laughter, and memories, all of which have excellent health benefits!

Yes, there are challenges, but those are hardly permanent. And it is these challenges that bring about growth. So when you feel overwhelmed by guilt, doubt, fear, or worry, turn on your gratitude switch and alter your internal dialogue from *Was I too harsh? Did I spend enough time with my kids this week? Did I do my best?* to *I'm grateful to be here to support my children. I'm grateful that I care enough to want to spend more time with them. I know I'll do better next week. I'm grateful to have these beautiful children.*

Gratitude is a great perspective shifter, and one way that we can all easily invite it in is by having a quick, personal parenting gratitude affirmation. It could be a favorite quote or a sentence you make up that resonates for you. The statement *I am grateful for my beautiful children, despite the challenges* adjusts my attitude to one of gratitude every time. I try to remind myself of it right before I'm about to tackle a pressing parental dilemma. And when I forget, life shows up—for example, in the form of my friend who lost his son—to remind me of it.

Another practice that can work wonders is taking a minute to make a gratitude list. Listing the top three blessings in your life can help tweak our outlook and put things back in perspective really fast. Or you can keep a daily journal, starting each page with the heading *I am grateful for* . . . There are even smartphone apps for it. I've turned to my gratitude app at many a down time and made a conscious effort to use expressions of gratitude to shift my perspective. It works every time.

And if it is your kids who are sad, mad, disappointed, or just in a complaining mood, charge up your Parental Guidance System, practice Dealing with the Feeling, give them a big hug, and then turn up the background music and help them tune in to the soothing notes of gratitude. Encourage them to make their own gratitude journals, and urge them to write their own gratitude affirmation. These practices will strengthen their internal and external communication habits while sprinkling musical notes of joy into their lives.

The Musical Notes of Unconditional Love

Like gratitude, unconditional love can form an underlying melody that adds harmony and beauty to our lives. Unconditional love means loving completely, and we love completely when the love that we feel in our hearts flows through our expressions, actions, and body language into the heart of another. In the depths of our hearts, we all love our kids unconditionally. They may make us mad or disappoint us at times, but we love them all the same. If they make a mistake, we don't love them any less.

Nevertheless, after kids have made a mistake, they might say to their parents, *You don't love me.* Why? Often the language we use unintentionally sends confusing messages to our children. *How could you be so stupid?* we say. *That's really dumb. What is wrong with you?* With words like these, we devalue and mislead our kids. We make them feel stupid or dumb or that something is wrong with them. And that makes them doubt themselves and our unconditional love for them. This doubt weakens our communication and our relationship with our kids, despite our unconditionally loving intentions.

When children make mistakes, recognize the difference between who they are and what they have done. By directing attention toward their negative behavior instead of toward them personally, we teach with empathy and compassion. In *The Gifts of Imperfection*, researcher and professor Dr. Brené Brown says, "When we're looking for compassion, we need someone who is deeply rooted, is able to bend and, most of all, embraces us for our strengths and struggles."[25] For our kids, we are the ones who can offer them that compassion and that unconditional love by putting our love for them *first*.

Empathy and Compassion

These two heartwarming notes help us deliver the music of unconditional love to the hearts of our children. There is nothing complicated about being empathetic and compassionate. It simply means that when we are upset at our children, we need to, first and foremost, remember to put ourselves in their shoes. When we do that, our response to the issue automatically becomes compassionate or kind, which helps us get the message across more productively.

As we've discussed, by directing anger toward our kids, we hurt their feelings and charge up their emotional temperature, which prevents us from tapping into their intellect and reasoning with them. This only leads to emotional and communication breakdowns, which affect their self-esteem, self-worth, and self-confidence, while leaving us with guilt and doubt.

If you need to use a firm tone of voice (say, if some challenging issue is a recurring one), by all means, do it. That's your call. But be empathetic and compassionate while doing it. Choose your words so that, despite the issue, the kids still feel the notes of your unconditional love—for example, "I know you are a smart kid, but what you *did* was not smart at all. Please explain what happened." This kind of mindful response keeps children's hearts and minds open to sharing the details with you. It also keeps them open to learning from the mistake.

Empathy always precedes compassion. When we are empathetic, we are compassionate; one goes hand in hand with the other. And in the end, there is less emotion commotion, the kids recover faster, and they still feel our unconditional love and support.

Health guru Dr. Mehmet Oz says that the opposite of anger is not calmness; it is empathy. If we take a second to put that into practice, it becomes crystal clear that empathy is what ushers calmness into an angry situation. Compassion, then, follows right at its heels, soothing the emotion commotion and firing up our PGS—holding our hand so we can move quickly toward a resolution.

Dr. Jill Bolte Taylor, a Harvard-trained neuroanatomist, teaches the "ninety-second emotion rule" in her enlightening book, *My Stroke of Insight*. She says that it takes less than ninety seconds for an emotion to be triggered, surge chemically through our bloodstream, and then get flushed out. She adds that even an extreme emotion cannot last more than ninety seconds, if we just let it be. After that, she says, anything we feel is of our own choosing.

Let's remember that when we are upset. At the height of a negative emotion, take a ninety-second time-out: Take nine deep breaths, drink nine slow sips of water, or simply ask yourself, "How would I feel if I were my child right now?" Contemplate the answer for the remainder of the time, and you will feel your emotion dissipate. I have tried and timed these ninety-second emotional management techniques, and they have yet to fail me.

By riding out our own emotions, we don't succumb to them— instead we calmly pass through them. What an effective way to put love first! Once we have done that, we completely change our own emotional landscape and our response, delivering the music of unconditional love to the ears and hearts of our children, which is where it rightfully belongs.

If we don't make our unconditional love clear and felt, the hurtful results will affect both us and our children for years to come. "In my teen years, when I messed up, my own mother was far from empathetic or compassionate," one mom remembered.

> She would not only tell me that I was stupid or dumb but she would also compare me to a neighbor's kid or a cousin. It infuriated me and made me feel like no matter how "good" I tried to be, I still was not good enough. Her reactions and words shut me down completely. So I started to ignore her and did whatever I wanted to do, behind her back more

often than not. I got into a lot of trouble because I felt that she didn't understand me. I felt unloved.

By sixteen years of age, I had low self-confidence, and I made a lot of stupid mistakes that affected me, my grades, my family, and my friendships. I know now that my mother did love me, but I sure didn't feel that at the time that I most needed it.

Now, when I deal with issues with my own kids, I try to remember how that felt, so I can do it differently. I realize how important it is to understand what my kids are feeling and to choose my words so they don't end up feeling lost the way I did or make the mistakes that I made. I learned the hard way. For years, I didn't even respect my mother, because I felt like she didn't deserve it—or maybe because she didn't ever make me feel like she understood me or respected *my* feelings.

This mom's example has stayed with me because it's a clear testimony of why empathy and compassion are such important elements of unconditional love. When we are empathetic, we put ourselves in our kid's shoes and understand his or her perspective before we utter a word. I'm positive that this mom's mother loved her daughter unconditionally, but unfortunately, in her daughter's all-important teen years, she failed to express it, which is why her daughter failed to feel it. That hurt her daughter's self-esteem, took her down the wrong road, broke down their communication, and hindered their relationship.

When the musical notes of our unconditional love are audible to our kids, they learn their lessons quickly and bounce back faster; they are more secure and confident. All in all, they are happier and we are happier, which makes us enjoy one another more.

Parental Discretion Advised

The emotions between parent and child may not be the only commotion that our children are exposed to. When parents disagree with each other, go through a divorce, or feud with grandparents, aunts, uncles, and cousins, the children are watching and soaking it all in. This is the time to put *love first* by using the natural filter of parental discretion. Unconditional love for your children also means shielding them from your own emotional commotion over other issues. Remove the kids from pressing issues that have nothing to do with them. Don't expose them to the toxicity of adult problems before their time.

"I am guilty of that," admitted a mom, "and I have seen the effects come back to bite me." She explained:

> I had a disagreement with my sister-in-law, and we had it out in front of the family. All the kids—hers and mine—started crying. What a mess! It took time and energy to explain to the kids what had happened and why. When all was said and done, we thought we had helped settle the kids' emotions.
>
> But the following week, over something very minor, my ten-year-old daughter started to scream at her other cousin, who was shocked and immediately started howling. Since this was very out of character for my daughter, I decided to nip it in the bud. "You were rude and disrespectful, and you

scared her. You know this is unacceptable behavior in our house." Without any hesitation, she responded, "How come when you yelled at Aunty A in this house, it was acceptable?"

Children's minds are not developed enough to comprehend the complexities of adult emotional breakdowns. They are just learning to manage their own emotions. No matter how upset or mad you are, if it has nothing to do with the kids, keep the children out of it. Live the mantra that you want them to have: *Family—immediate and extended—is important. Love rules.* There is no better way to exemplify self-control and emotional management than by practicing it yourself. We can be the absolute best parent to our child, but when we disrespect our own parents, relatives, or friends, our kids will follow suit.

Compassion, empathy, and parental discretion are all notes of unconditional love. When we combine them, they become a synchronized harmony that is part of our children's inner music, their inner perfection, for the rest of their lives.

The Musical Notes of Letting Go

One of our greatest human gifts is that we have the ability to let go of unnecessary thoughts and emotions, and yet that is one of our least-used gifts. When we let go, we release ourselves from the emotion commotion and replace that noise with the background music that makes our experiences more enjoyable and memorable.

By no means does letting go of negativity mean that your life will be devoid of challenges. But it will definitely tilt your intellectual, emotional, and physical responses away from stress, worry, guilt, doubt, and fear. Letting go of things shortens the duration of the emotion commotion. If you're having trouble getting there, *reflection* will help you *redirect* your emotions and *reconnect* with your inner perfection. Like gratitude, letting go is also a powerful mood elevator. It helps release the trapped emotion, freeing up internal space, making more room for us to be happy, think positive, and do good.

"I completely get that," said one mom in my class. "But what happens when my child has been bullied or pushed in school? Am I supposed to just let go of that? If I didn't do anything about it, I think I would be setting a bad example for my child, and it would make us feel worse."

Letting go does not mean being ignorant of what's going on around you. Not standing up for yourself or your child, or not addressing the issue when your child has been hurt or bullied, is unacceptable behavior by every parent. However, after you have addressed the issue with the school authorities, neighbors, friends, or whoever was responsible, and after you have reached a satisfactory resolution, then let it go. Drop it. Too often after we've done our best to clean up the mess at hand, we continue building the emotion commotion. We keep on discussing what happened, over and over again, magnifying emotions already past and creating a new challenging situation that's more draining than the original issue.

When my son was nine years old, he carelessly strolled in front of a friend who was practicing hits with a metal baseball bat. And . . . *wham*!

The bat barely grazed his face, but Navin still ended up with a dent in the bone of his upper left cheek. The doctors told us how lucky we were that no facial bones were broken, but he had a big bruise on his cheek for over a month. During that time, every person who saw him would ask, "What happened?" And I would repeat the story. By the end of a fortnight, my son was healing quite well, but I was exhausted! My neck, back, and jaw had been stiff for two weeks, and I was beat. I wondered why. After all, besides what ended up looking like a dimple, no permanent damage was done. I was very grateful that Navin was okay. So why was I so tired?

The following day, a distant relative who had heard the story from another family member called me to see if Navin was okay. "I heard that he got hit by a baseball bat and has broken his cheekbone," she said. Instinctively, not wanting to repeat the exhausting story one more time, I answered, "No, no. His cheekbone did not break, thank God. And he is fine—thanks for asking. He now has what looks like the cutest dimple on his left cheek!" We both laughed and caught up on other things.

Later that evening, I happened to answer my mother-in-law's phone, and when her friend on the other end of the line heard my voice, she immediately said, "I heard about Navin. I was so worried. Is he okay?" This time I decided, a little more consciously, not to repeat the entire story and instead stuck to the *He's fine, thank God, and he now has a cute dimple* response.

Then my sister, who had been out of town, called and said, "I heard! Oh my, is he okay?" Once again I stuck to my shorter response.

The next day I woke up with no neck, back, or jaw pain, and my energy level was back to normal. What had been exhausting me, I realized, was that I had repeated this story unnecessarily hundreds of times, and it had taken a toll on me.

My mom always said, "When you let go, you welcome good—good feelings, good thoughts, and good health." Sure enough, as I let go of repetitively reliving the story, I started to feel good and my energy level rose. I started to heal.

When we get caught up in unnecessary, self-created drama, we are building a trap for ourselves. By simply narrating the brighter side of the story, I felt much lighter and relieved. I noticed that it was only when I consciously decided to let go of the story, that the story lost its hold on me, and I started to feel good. Interestingly enough, my son was also back to full speed a few days later. The lesson: Try not to hold on to negative breakdown emotions any longer than necessary. It's the only way to move on to the next step: forgiveness.

Forgiveness and Apologies

"My husband's brother said some really mean things to my mother-in-law about my husband," a mom in my class said. "Although my husband seems fine with it since my brother-in-law apologized for his irrational comments, I cannot seem to let it go. And it's been six months." We all can relate to that. It's not always easy to forgive and forget. When it comes to mending relationships, however, a big part of rebuilding comes from forgiveness. Forgiveness allows us to bypass resentments and grudges. When we forgive, we don't *give in* to a situation, we *give up* the situation. Forgiveness offers the opportunity to give up the emotion commotion by conscious choice. Through forgiveness we access our higher selves; we show off our inner perfection.

And if you're caught up in a taxing situation that you can't seem to leave behind, try Dealing with the Feeling: Spot it, say it, okay it, and then move to resolve it. In this particular case, I suggested the mom try: *I feel angry at my brother-in-law for talking behind my husband's back. It's okay for me to feel this way, because his actions hurt my feelings.*

Now move on and resolve the emotion: *Since my brother-in-law has apologized, and my husband has forgiven him, I need to do the same.* Remember that forgiveness is not a sign of weakness. If anything, it's a shining example of true strength in character—one you want to exemplify to your kids. Forgiveness does not change the past, but it definitely brightens the present and future.

Ever notice that when we hold on to detrimental internal emotions, our family and our kids bear the brunt of it? Why waste your precious life and moments with your family over a petty situation? Let go, forgive, and move on. "Forgiveness is a funny thing," said inspirational writer William Arthur Ward. "It warms the heart and cools the sting."

When we forgive, we let go and let goodness back into our lives. After kids have messed up and then apologized, let the topic go. Continually reminding them about it simply starts the emotion commotion back up. Forgiveness supports effective parenting and places the focus back on whatever important lesson you want your kids to learn.

On the same note, when you have made a mistake, apologize willingly and wholeheartedly to your kids, whatever their age. One is never too old or too proud to apologize or to be humble when a mistake is made. When we say, *I'm sorry,* we reclaim love; we put love first. As Craig Silvey, the Australian novelist said in *Jasper Jones*, "Sorry doesn't take things back, but it pushes them forward. It bridges the gap. Sorry is a sacrament. It's an offering. A gift."[26]

As every parent knows, kids of any age are quick to forgive. Kids innately know, much better than adults do, how to quickly let go. Be like your kids. Learn that from them. Let go. It will encourage your children to do the same with their friends, family members, and future relationships, building long-term positive habits.

Guide and Step Aside

When my kids were halfway through their junior year of high school, we started to notice their struggle for independence. As talks of college applications became more frequent, the idea of leaving home and taking care of themselves understandably grew more real to them. They both pushed for easier curfews and for the freedom to make more of their own decisions. Even though they had started driving and were beginning to break out of our constant supervision and direction, it was tough for my husband and me to let go.

Sometimes I would say, "I think it's too soon to let her go completely. After all, she is only seventeen. She has just started driving."

My husband would reply, "You have to start now. It's good preparation for going off to college."

At other times, especially after one of them had made a mistake, my husband would say, "Maybe he is not ready to manage his own life completely yet. Let's give him independence in small chunks and see how he does."

"We have to start letting go now," I would respond, "so he can fall and learn while he is still at home and we are around to help him get back up."

There is no one correct answer. Giving our children their independence and letting go of them step by step has to be based on each child's personality. While they're under our wing, we must give our children more room to be independent. This is the only way we can be reassured that they will be able to take care of themselves when they do leave home.

Letting go of our children is one of the biggest challenges that parents face. It is particularly difficult when we experience, firsthand, the transition of our teenage children into young adults. The only way we can show them our unconditional love at this age is by keeping the doors of communication wide open and reminding ourselves to *guide and step aside.* Even though this can be the most trying part of raising children, it's the only way to prepare them to thrive on their own. Yes, they will stall and fall, but this will also teach them to stand tall. Stay at arm's length, watch them closely, and stay out of their way—not to let go completely but to step aside and watch from the sidelines. Stepping into young adulthood is a process of self-discovery for them. If our kids want to be the captains of their own ships, we have to be prepared to be the co-captains and be there to help them navigate through the big waves.

When they do fall, curb yourself from saying anything resembling *I told you so* or from calling them "irresponsible." Instead, put your unconditional love into words by saying, "That's okay. This is how you will learn to take care of yourself and become more responsible. I know this hurts," you might say. "I've been there. But this is how you will learn. I know you can do this."

Encourage them to learn from their mistakes. Help them get back on their feet, and then hand over the steering wheel again. *Guide and step aside* is a parenting model that every parent should practice. It is the ultimate expression of letting go and of unconditional love—one that nurtures their resilience and self-reliance and anchors their inner perfection.

Laugh, Sing, Dance, Hug

The eighteenth-century English poet Lord Byron said, "Always laugh when you can. It's cheap medicine." Laughter helps us let go and rise above the emotion commotion; it uplifts the mood and injects fun into ordinary challenges.

A mom in my class, who has a great sense of humor, shared a cute story:

> The other day, I was furious at my husband over a heated family issue that put us on opposite sides.

And I could tell that he was not going to apologize. He called home to ask about an upcoming parent-teacher conference so he could pencil the date into his work calendar. Although my first instinct was to hang up on him, I gave him the date, and then he started making small talk.

"Are you still mad?" he asked, "because you know, it's not my fault, and I'm not going to apologize."

I was about to burst, but in an effort to refrain from using a curse word, since the kids were around and he was at work, I said, "HAPPY BIRTHDAY!" in an unmistakably mean tone of voice.

"What do you mean?" he asked.

I repeated, "Happy birthday!"—this time adding a sarcastic undertone.

"Well, haaaapy birthday to you, too!" he snapped back.

"No, haaaaapy birthdaaaay to YOU!" I responded.

The next thing we knew, we were both laughing out loud. And then he surprised me with, "Hey, I'm sorry. I should have stood up for you." When he got home that day, he was in a great mood and told me that my *Happy birthday!* had gone viral in his office. He shared the story with one of his colleagues, and within a couple of hours, people were walking around randomly substituting *Happy birthday!* for sarcasm and anger.

Make up family phrases like *Happy birthday!* to substitute for inappropriate words or simply to infuse humor and brighten dark attitudes—your own, your spouse's, and your children's. My husband interrupts my anger (or my kids' anger) with an endless train of *I love you . . . I love you . . . I love you.* It always makes us laugh and sets free whatever bee is in our bonnet.

Along with laughter, singing, dancing, and hugs are all cheap medicine. Dr. Jay Kumar, in his book *Brain, Body, and Being,* refers to *laughter, singing,* and *dancing* as the LSD for the Soul! This natural concoction serves a dual purpose: It simultaneously and instantly dispels negative energy and propels positive energy. The contagious, therapeutic, wholesome pheromones of this drug of the soul push us toward optimum health and inner well-being. And the music, joy, and memories left behind are momentous.

"So these are all communication tools, too?" asked a dad. Well, of course they are! Letting go is another key musical note in enjoyable and memorable parenting, which unlocks the door to communication between parents and children.

The Musical Notes of Inspiration

The great scientist Albert Einstein said, "Imagination is everything. It is the preview of life's coming attractions." Needless to say, young kids have no shortage of imagination. If anything, they have a surplus of it. Parents are the first ones whom kids pick to share their imaginative ideas with—because they trust us and they believe we will help and support them in turning their imaginations into reality.

I was inspired when I read the story of Caine's Arcade. Thanks to his father's encouragement, nine-year-old Caine Monroy had built an arcade out of cardboard in his father's auto parts store. A filmmaker happened to stop by for a door handle, took a few turns at the play arcade, and was awed by this child's vision. He made a film that inspired innovation and eventually led to his starting the Imagination Foundation, whose mission is to "find, foster and fund creativity and entrepreneurship in kids." Today, the Imagination Foundation nurtures and encourages thousands of young innovators and problem solvers to pursue their dreams.

Even though the arcade was Caine's idea, the boy's very first inspiration was encouraged by his father. We are placed in our kids' lives to encourage and inspire their dreams and aspirations. Through inspiration, we can touch their spirit.

Think about the word *inspire,* whose root means to "breathe life into." Inspiring kids means making the time to breathe life into their imagination. Take a quick trip to the art supply store . . . rummage for supplies from the garage . . . or give them some cardboard, tape, and scissors. Sometimes that's all the encouragement kids need to get started.

Each child comes into this world bearing his or her own gifts to share. For your children, it could be a personal passion or a little idea they want to transform into a larger one. It's your job to encourage them, support them, and help them do it.

Discover what your children's dreams are. One fun way of doing this is to create a dream board with your children. You can begin by asking them five questions that represent the five spokes on the wheel of life:

1. What would you love to do when you grow up (career)?

2. How would you like to help others (community)?

3. What activity or sport do you love (health)?

4. Which people do you love and would you love to have in your life (family and friends)?

5. What qualities do you love about yourself, and what qualities would you like to grow in yourself (inner well-being)?

Help them write down their answers and start cutting out pictures from magazines to support those answers, and just start pasting them on the board. If your child is old enough to make his or her own dream board, make one for yourself along with them—or turn it into a fun activity for the whole family.

Dream boards are a great tool for inner exploration and communication. They help children brainstorm and express their thoughts. They nurture young minds to think imaginatively and freely, and they inspire older kids and teenagers to home in on what excites them. Dream boards inspire us at any age to realize our vision—which is both satisfying and joyful to our souls. "Cherish your visions and your dreams, as they are the children of your soul, the blueprints of your ultimate achievements," said Napoleon Hill, a pioneer of the New Thought movement.

I was taken by the words of Nancy Giordano, Chief Idea Wrangler of TEDxAustin, at a talk that I attended: "We are in an age of contribution, not extraction," she said. What does she mean by that? I think in recent generations, parents were more focused on extracting the best out of their children through academics. If we were good at math, science, or language, they took that talent and made it the road map to our future. People my age typically were encouraged to become service professionals—doctors, lawyers, engineers, teachers. Entrepreneurs were few and far between.

Today things are different. Thanks to technology, our kids are exposed to endless choices. They are more open-minded about personal possibilities and place fewer boundaries on what they can accomplish. They dream big! Not contributing to those dreams is detrimental to their well-being, their inner spirit, and their self-confidence. A mom who has teenage kids told me that her fifteen-year-old son wants to major in computer science, and his dream is to be a software engineer, but he's not so good at math. She said,

"I always discourage him by reminding him that he has to love, be good at, and get good grades in math in order to get there. It's a fact, isn't it? Wouldn't I be setting him up for disappointment and failure if I encourage him in that direction?"

Maybe not. In a 2011 *New York Times* article, Vivek Wadhwa, a former senior research associate at Harvard Law School and the current director of research at the Center for Entrepreneurship at Duke University, wrote, "I have interviewed the founders of more than 200 Silicon Valley start-ups. The most common traits I have observed are a passion to change the world and the confidence to defy the odds and succeed."[27]

Actualizing their dreams requires that our children harbor a passion that surpasses all theoretical requirements. It's a parent's job to add fuel to that fire of our children's passions, to encourage them and support them and tell them that they can be whomever and whatever they aspire to be. Would it not be more heartwarming and encouraging for your kids to hear, "Of course I think you will be a great software engineer. Just a little more focus on math, and you're there!" Then do what you need to do, as a parent, to help them—tutors, extra practice, whatever it takes. This will keep their self-confidence intact as they continue to work toward their goals.

The poem "Children Learn What They Live," by Dorothy Nolte, offers parents a powerful line: "If children live with encouragement, they learn confidence." When we encourage our children to surrender to their passion, we inspire them to get closer to their own greatness. This is how we teach them to be confident. That should be our contribution.

Sure, their passion might not translate into a career path. Sometimes it stays alive as a hobby, though. My daughter, Nitasha, loves to explore the world through her camera lens, and though for her career she joined the marketing department of the family business, she has found a way to use her passion for photography in other ways for the firm's benefit. One year for our company Christmas party, she spent weeks of her own time preparing a fun video about the company culture and the personalities of the staff. She called it "The Office," and it was such a hit, so full of laughter and love, that it has now become an annual company tradition.

Often, when my husband and I see her passion for these creative projects come to life, we ask if she wants to reconsider and pursue a career in photography. Her answer is always the same: "For now, it's my hobby." As Sir Ken Robinson would put it, it's her *element*. In his best-selling book of that name, he defines the "element" as "the point at which natural talent meets personal passion." It's the place where people "feel most themselves, most inspired, and achieve at the highest levels."[28]

Of course, we want our children to achieve to their fullest potential. For some children, their passion and vision will be clear from the onset; they want to be doctors or scientists or artists or athletes or entrepreneurs. For others, we as parents have to be observant if we are to discover what they are passionate about, and then we have to help them pursue it. Sometimes we have to dig around to figure out what they love and help them find ways to enjoy it—even if only as a hobby. As Robinson says, "Human resources are like natural resources; they're often buried deep. You have to go looking for them; they're not always lying around on the surface. You have to create the circumstances where they show themselves." Create those circumstances so your kids can realize and showcase their inner elements. Be that conduit for them.

And if *you* have an idea, a buried desire, or a passion for something, be sure to inspire and encourage yourself to follow your dreams, too. Make time for it. There is no better example to set for your children. I know that life gets so busy with the must-do's of raising kids, building careers, maintaining households, and meeting family obligations that there seems to be very little time for anything else. But I promise you, if you can incorporate what inspires you into your daily life for only a few minutes a day, it will do wonders for your soul. It will make you better at your career, a better parent, and a happier human being. Following your passion will bring the music of joy into your life and into your family.

Last year, a coworker and friend approached me and said, "Lately, I've been getting in creative jams. I'll be in the middle of a project, and my brain just stops. I'll circle around the problem for an hour, but I find myself getting only more frustrated and less productive. I need some inspiration! Any suggestions?"

I knew this friend used to play the guitar, so I asked him if he had ever recorded any of his own pieces.

"Yes!" he said.

"Well, bring that piece to work and play it when you're in a jam. Put on some earphones if you need to. Use the music that you created to inspire your creative work here. It will help you reconnect with your creative side."

He called me the next day and told me that the idea had worked. Though he might never have thought of it, channeling his creativity through his own passion—music—had pulled him back into a creative flow at work.

Our passions can help us do that, even if they are separate from what we do for a living. They can help us get back to being productive, feeling good, and inspiring ourselves.

There is something amazing about being a source of inspiration for our children: That inspiration helps contribute to the collective future of the world our children will grow up in. When we inspire our children to be or do what they are passionate about, we help them multiply their passion and share it with others. And when we, the parents, get to be a part of the process, it fills our minutes, hours, months, years, and life with immense pride, joy, and cherished memories.

Making Memories Count

Before we know it, our kids are all grown up. They've spread their wings, claimed their independence, and entered the next phase of busy-ness in their lives. As young adults, their focus is ahead, not behind. In a parallel way, we parents now have a new focus—a new chunk of time to fill. We no longer spend each day dropping them off, picking them up, taking them to practices, attending sports and school events, preparing meals, or helping them sort out everyday issues. Now we parent from a distance.

Yes, we may get excited about how we are going to spend this "free" time—focusing on our career or our passions, taking dance or language lessons, working out, traveling, or socializing more. However, the absence of our children unquestionably leaves a void in our home and our heart. We face the proverbial empty nest. At times like this, what makes us feel better? What puts a smile on our face? Memories. It is memories that fill our hearts with flashbacks of the fun times, the challenging times, the laughs, and the friendships. We reach out for the pictures, albums, collages, and videos, and we spend umpteen hours in reflection, reliving the good times. Our fond memories of times with our kids give us lots to reminisce about.

We all want these types of memories. Every parent wants to recollect their children's childhood with a sense of pride and self-accomplishment. But the fact is—and we all know this—those memories can bring either tears of happiness and joy or tears of regret and sadness. Happiness will reign if we have enjoyed the ride, continue to maintain a good relationship with our kids, and believe we did the best job we could. Regret and sadness will rule if we missed out on the joy that this parenting ride has to offer, if we worry that our ongoing relationship with our kids is not as strong as we might like, if we fear that they might not turn to us anymore—or, most of all, if we feel guilty that we didn't pay more attention to this most important job we'll ever do.

That certainly does not have to be you. Empowered by these Tools of Growth, your Parental Guidance System is ready to go. Play the background music of Enjoyable and Memorable Parenting. Use Honorable, Approachable, Sensible, and Reasonable and Responseable Parenting—and your innate parental instinct—to open wide the doors of communication with your kids. Tap into your inner perfection. Build trust and confidence in yourselves and your children, and teach them by example how to stay connected, be happy, think positive, and do good.

This is how you can enjoy the ride and create memories that will fill your lives with infinite joy long after your children have left your nest.

We spend the prime years of our lives grooming our children for their grand, independent entry into the real world. This is the moment we have prepared for all these years. And when it arrives, we want to feel that this truly is just the beginning of a different phase of our relationship with our perfect precious ones. We want to be confident that *we* have done well, and to trust that *they* will do well. That's really all that every parent wants for their kids. Because, we know in our hearts, when all is said and done, that our treasure is the memories that we create together. Our wealth is not the cars we drive or the money we have in our bank account. Our wealth is our children and our family.

In joy!

Affirmation Reminder

I enjoy being a parent and am rewarded every day with the memories I am given and those I give.

I am the "perfect" parent, who uses these tools of growth to raise my child to be happy, think positive, and do good.

 Quick Takeaways

- The musical note of gratitude boosts the self-worth, self-esteem, self-confidence, and happiness of both the giver and the receiver.

- Empathy, compassion, and parental discretion are all melodious notes of unconditional love. When we combine them, they become part of our children's inner music for the rest of their lives.

- Forgive, apologize, and let go to release negative breakdown emotions and make more room for goodness to shine through.

- Guide and step aside. This nurtures resilience and self-reliance, preparing your kids to thrive on their own.

- Laugh, sing, dance, and hug! Do at least one of these every day. They are instant mood elevators.

- Encourage and inspire your children's dreams and aspirations. They are the future.

- Create memories that will fill your heart with pride and joy for the rest of your life.

The "Perfect" Parent Toolbox

Sometimes in our busy lives, we just need a quick fix. This easy-access toolbox will help you by:

1. Serving as a quick parenting refresher to tighten up your communication habits, when and as needed;

2. Reminding you of the essential communication tools; and

3. Giving you simple talking points to share the love with other parents.

Introduction

 Affirmation Reminder

I am the "perfect" parent for my child! I use my inner perfection to connect
with my kids.

Get Ready for a Parenting Makeover

 Affirmation Reminder

Each day, through good communication, I am building a great relationship
with my child.

 Quick Takeaways

- By shifting your perspective you can give yourself a parenting makeover.

- Tuning in requires memorizing your goal—a great relationship with your
  kids—and knowing that it is important to align your actions with that goal.

- Effective communication is the bridge that aligns our actions with
  our parenting goal.

- Use your Parental Guidance System (PGS)—your innate parental instinct
  and your communication tools.

Tool #1. Honorable Parenting: Planting Self-Confidence

 Affirmation Reminder

I am an Honorable and confident parent doing the best that I can. I accept and respect myself and my child just as we are.

 Quick Takeaways

- Accept and respect yourself and your child—feelings included.

- The Communication Balance is the balance of your thoughts and feelings (inner communication landscape), which leads to your expressions (outer communication landscape).

Communication Balance

Thoughts + Feelings (inner communication landscape)

↓

Expressions (outer communication landscape)

- Effective communication means balancing your thoughts and your feelings to guide your expressions.

- To fast-forward into balanced and effective communication, as often as you can, practice **Dealing with the Feeling** with yourself and your child:

  ✓ **Spot it**—identify the feeling (anger, sadness, hurt, etc.)

  ✓ **Say it**—say the feeling out loud ("I know you're feeling angry.")

  ✓ **Okay it**—validate it ("I understand how you must be feeling. If my brother broke my toy, I would feel the same way too.")

  Now, move to resolve.

Tool #2. Approachable Parenting: Growing Trust

 Affirmation Reminder

I am an Approachable and trusted parent. I listen with an open mind and an open heart, guiding my children and empowering them to learn and grow from their mistakes.

 Quick Takeaways

- Take Five. Give yourself five uninterrupted minutes each day to do nothing with your child. This is the ultimate communication reset tool.

- Be flexible and creative. Listen with an open mind and allow your children to complete their thought. Be open to change and growth, and your children will learn to do the same. If you're not getting through to your child, try a different approach.

- Set guidelines instead of rules. This encourages structure and engages children's intellect and decision-making skills, which fosters independence.

- Let the grounding fit the deed, and, as much as possible, be consistent and follow through.

- Encourage children to make a "What did I learn from this mistake?" list. It helps recovery and growth.

Tool #3. Sensible Parenting: Nurturing Connections

 Affirmation Reminder

I am a Sensible and nurturing parent. I use my five senses to see beyond the obvious, be attentive to my child's inner needs, and deliver the love that I feel.

 Quick Takeaways

- Make "sense" of an emotional situation by using your senses.

- Make eye contact to let your children see and feel that you acknowledge and understand their point of view.

- Listen patiently to connect deeply. Let children complete their thoughts and sentences before offering suggestions, especially when you know they are wrong. And when you are right, practice being kind first.

- Smell situations or be perceptive before responding.

- Practice verbal hygiene to inspire respect from children. Use words that taste good to you and your child, and sprinkle in words of endearment. Then no matter what you are saying, it will be received positively.

- Touch their hearts by using your magical touch to communicate with children.

- Take five deep breaths and sips of water to activate your senses and your PGS when you're challenged. This will buy some time to help calm your emotions, bring clarity to your thoughts, and turn a reaction into a well-thought-out response.

Tool #4. Reasonable and Responsible Parenting: Branching Out through Understanding

 Affirmation Reminder

I am a Reasonable, Responsible, and understanding parent. I am a calm and kind voice of reason who encourages open communication and loving emotional expression.

 Quick Takeaways

- Be the calm and kind voice of reason. A simple *Why? What?* or *How?* can turn an emotional discussion into a productive intellectual discussion.

- Respond intelligently instead of reacting emotionally, facilitating a communication balance. Reasoning deepens understanding and bypasses arguments; responses trump reactions.

- If you have *reacted impulsively*, reflect, redirect, and reconnect to put yourself back on the path to being response-able and open the door to communication. Be willing to apologize—it helps redirect the discussion toward progress.

- Use open-ended questions to start the conversation and to extract answers that go beyond *Yes, No,* and *I don't know*.

- Our expressions become our children's impressions. An emotional legacy of robust expressions of love and happiness is what every parent wants to pass on through our children to future generations.

Tool #5. Enjoyable and Memorable Parenting: Reaping the Fruits

 Affirmation Reminder

I enjoy being a parent and am rewarded every day with the memories I am given and those I give.

 Quick Takeaways

- The musical note of gratitude boosts the self-worth, self-esteem, self-confidence, and happiness of both the giver and the receiver.

- Empathy, compassion, and parental discretion are all melodious notes of unconditional love. When we combine them, they become part of our children's inner music for the rest of their lives.

- Forgive, apologize, and let go to release negative breakdown emotions and make more room for goodness to shine through.

- Guide and step aside. This nurtures resilience and self-reliance, preparing your kids to thrive on their own.

- Laugh, sing, dance, and hug! Do at least one of these every day. They are instant mood elevators.

- Encourage and inspire your children's dreams and aspirations. They are the future.

- Create memories that will fill your heart with pride and joy for the rest of your life.

Acknowledgments

Infinite love and gratitude to . . .

Julie Watson, my friend and Tools of Growth confidante. Thank you for believing in me and standing by my side. Your creativity, intelligence, and knowledge fuel my passion and anchor my purpose; your kindness warms my heart. This book and TOG have taken shape because of your guidance and support.

Tripta Khetarpal, my second mom and teacher. Your very presence in my daily life has finessed my communication habits and connected me deeply with the potential of my inner perfection.

Nitasha Khetarpal, my MVP! You have been by my side from day one—we began by signing the contract for this book together and we approved the last proofread together! Thank you for being my sounding board and for constantly reminding me to "have fun" through the process. I am awed by your unconditional love, perseverance, and wisdom.

Navin Khetarpal, my Zen master. Thank you for encouraging me to share with other parents many of the lessons I have learned from our journey together. Your larger-than-life presence, mindful words, and timely hugs have been my much-needed blessings.

Simi Gandhi, my soul sister. Your unconditional love and encouragement always pushes me to jump higher. I worship the beautiful friend that you are.

My family—my brother, sisters, nieces, and nephews. Sharing our celebrations and overcoming our challenges has allowed me to test drive the communication tools outlined in this book. Thank you for your trust and faith.

Bill Wallen. You are proof that there are no accidents. You showed up in perfect time. Thank you for being able to envision this book and for introducing me to Greenleaf Book Group.

Greenleaf Book Group. What a talented team of professionals—the perfect orchestra to create my music with! It was a pleasure and honor to have worked with each one of you. And I have a feeling that this is just the beginning.

Aaron Hierholzer, my concertmaster and "perfect" friend. You far surpassed your commitment as my in-house editor. Thank you for carrying me through the ups and the downs of this new endeavor with your calm and kind voice of reason.

Joan Tapper, my talented editor and friend. I struck gold the very first time—how lucky I am! Your impeccable wisdom and expertise has skillfully extracted the very best from within me, shaping this book, all the while preserving my voice. Sorry, you are stuck with me for life.

Lacie Romano, my friend and TOG fan. Five years ago you said this would happen, and here we are. Like a beautiful rainbow you, too, showed up at the perfect time, to add color to this project. Your talented eye brought to life many design elements for both the book and the website. I'm ever so grateful for your selfless love and endless hours of dedication.

The thought leaders of positive psychology, child development, and sociology. Thank you for giving me the science to back up my work and inspiring the ideas that have shaped this book.

My Happy Relaxed Parents. Look where your love and support has brought me! Thank you for believing in me and my TOG message. Thank you, too, for opening your hearts, sharing your personal parental moments, and giving me a launching pad. I love you all dearly. This is your book, not mine!

Recommended Reading

Andersen, Uell S., *Three Magic Words*.

Brett, Regina, *Be The Miracle: 50 Lessons for Making the Impossible Possible*.

Brown, Brené, *The Gifts of Imperfect Parenting* (audio book).

Carter, Christine, *Raising Happiness: 10 Simple Steps for More Joyful Kids and Happier Parents*.

Chapman, Gary, and Ross Campbell, *The Five Love Languages of Children*.

Covey, Stephen, *The 7 Habits of Highly Effective People*.

Dweck, Carol, *Mindset: The New Psychology of Success*.

Dyer, Wayne, *The Power of Intention*.

Farber, Edward, *Raising the Kid You Love with the Ex You Hate*.

Galinsky, Ellen, *Mind in the Making: The Seven Essential Life Skills Every Child Needs*.

Gladwell, Malcolm, *Outliers: The Story of Success*.

Goleman, Daniel, *Emotional Intelligence: Why It Can Matter More Than IQ*.

Gopnik, Alison, *The Philosophical Baby: What Children's Minds Tell Us About Truth, Love, and the Meaning of Life*.

Gottman, John, *Raising an Emotionally Intelligent Child*.

Goulston, Mark, *Just Listen: Discover the Secret to Getting Through to Absolutely Anyone*.

Hanh, Thich Nhat, *True Love: A Practice for Awakening the Heart*.

Hewitt, Jonathan and Lana, *Life Ki-do Parenting: Tools to Raise Happy, Confident Kids from the Inside Out*.

Hiatt, Martha, *Mind Magic: Techniques for Transforming Your Life*.

His Holiness, the Dalai Lama, *In My Own Words: My Teachings and Philosophy*.

Keltner, Dacher, *Born to Be Good: The Science of a Meaningful Life.*

Kumar, Jay, *Brain, Body, and Being.*

Lipton, Bruce, *The Honeymoon Effect: The Science of Creating Heaven on Earth.*

McCloud, Carol, *Have You Filled a Bucket Today?*

Oswald, Yvonne, *Every Word Has Power: Switch on Your Language and Turn on Your Life.*

Parthasarathy, A., *Vedanta Treatise: The Eternities.*

Pert, Candace, *Molecules of Emotion: The Science of Mind-Body Medicine.*

Rath, Thomas, and Donald O. Clifton, *How Full Is Your Bucket?*

Robinson, Ken, *The Element: How Finding Your Passion Changes Everything.*

Rosenfeld, Alvin, *The Over-Scheduled Child: Avoiding the Hyper-Parenting Trap.*

Rubin, Gretchen, *The Happiness Project, or Why I Spent a Year Trying to Sing in the Morning, Clean My Closets, Fight Right, Read Aristotle, and Generally Have More Fun.*

Senn, Larry, *Up the Mood Elevator: Your Guide to Success Without Stress.*

Siegel, Daniel J., *Mindsight: The New Science of Personal Transformation.*

_____, and Mary Hartzell, *Parenting from the Inside Out: How a Deeper Self-Understanding Can Help You Raise Children Who Thrive.*

_____, and Tina Payne Bryson, *The Whole-Brain Child.*

Taylor, Jill Bolte, *My Stroke of Insight: A Brain Scientist's Personal Journey.*

Tolle, Eckhart, *A New Earth: Awakening to Your Life's Purpose.*

Tsabary, Shefali, *The Conscious Parent: Transforming Ourselves, Empowering Our Children.*

Walsch, Neale Donald, *When Everything Changes, Change Everything: In a Time of Turmoil, a Pathway to Peace.*

Wilber, Ken, *The Integral Vision: A Very Short Introduction to the Revolutionary Integral Approach to Life, God, the Universe, and Everything.*

Williamson, Marianne, *A Return to Love: Reflections on the Principles of A Course in Miracles.*

Zukav, Gary, *The Seat of the Soul.*

Notes

1   Associated Press, "Youth's Stuff of Happiness May Surprise Parents," NBCNews.com, August 20, 2007, http://www.nbcnews.com/id/20322621/#.UubQRXmqmjk.

2   Deepak Chopra, "Coincidences: Clues from the Universe," Beliefnet, October 2003, http://www.beliefnet.com/Wellness/2003/10/Coincidences-Clues-From-The-Universe-By-Deepak-Chopra.aspx#.

3   Description of Alvin Rosenfeld and Nicole Wise's *The Over-Scheduled Child*, http://www.hyper-parenting.com.

4   John Gottman, *Raising an Emotionally Intelligent Child* (New York: Simon & Schuster, 1997), p. 20.

5   Deepak Chopra, *The Seven Spiritual Laws of Yoga* (Hoboken, NJ: John Wiley & Sons, 2004), p. 32.

6   Daniel J. Siegel, *Mindsight* (New York: Bantam, 2011), p. xii.

7   Gretchen Rubin, *The Happiness Project* (New York: HarperCollins, 2009), p. 97.

8   Mayo Clinic Staff, "Relaxation Techniques: Try These Steps to Reduce Stress," May 19, 2011, http://www.mayoclinic.org/relaxation-technique/ART-20045368.

9   Cris Rowan, "The Impact of Technology on the Developing Child," *Huffington Post*, May 29, 2013, http://www.huffingtonpost.com/cris-rowan/technology-children-negative-impact_b_3343245.html.

10 Queen's University, "'Here's Looking at You' Has New Meaning: Eye Contact Shown to Affect Conversation Patterns, Group

Problem-Solving Ability," *ScienceDaily*, www.sciencedaily.com/
releases/2002/11/021122073858.htm.

11   Jodi Schulz, "Eye Contact: An Introduction to Its Role in
     Communication," Michigan State University Extension
     website, November 28, 2012, http://msue.anr.msu.edu/news/
     eye_contact_an_introduction_to_its_role_in_communication.

12   Kristyn Crow, "The Eyes Have It: How Eye Contact Can Transform
     Your Child," Families.com, August 3, 2006, http://www.families.com/
     blog/the-eyes-have-it-how-eye-contact-can-transform-your-child#.

13   Mark Goulston, "Promoting Self-Esteem with Active Listening,"
     Huffington Post, June 10, 2010, http://www.huffingtonpost.com/
     mark-goulston-md/active-listening-promotin_b_607720.html.

14   Jasper H. B. de Groot, Monique A. M. Smeets, Annemarie Kaldewaij,
     Maarten J. A. Duijndam, and Gün R. Semin, "Chemosignals
     Communicate Human Emotion," *Psychological Science* 23: 1417–1424.

15   Yvonne Oswald, *Every Word Has Power* (New York: Atria, 2008), back
     cover.

16   "You can either practice being right or practice being kind." Anne
     Lamott, *Plan B: Further Thoughts on Faith* (New York: Penguin, 2005),
     p. 97.

17   "When the choice is to be right or to be kind, always make the choice
     that brings peace," Dr. Wayne Dyer.

18   Bruce Lipton, *The Honeymoon Effect* (New York: Hay House, 2013),
     p. 84.

19   Dacher Keltner, "Hands On Research: The Science of Touch,"
     Greater Good Science Center Website, September 29, 2010, http://
     greatergood.berkeley.edu/article/item/hands_on_research.

20   "About Mindsight," Dr. Dan Siegel's website, http://www.drdansiegel
     .com/about/mindsight/.

21   "Over-reactive Parenting Linked to Negative Emotions and Problem
     Behavior in Toddlers," ScienceDaily, February 21, 2012, http://www
     .sciencedaily.com/releases/2012/02/120221103918.htm.

22 Debra Bradley Ruder, "The Teen Brain," *Harvard Magazine*, September–October 2008, http://harvardmagazine.com/2008/09/the-teen-brain.html.

23 Tina Payne Bryson and Daniel J. Siegel, "If I Had Bad Parents, Will I Be a Bad Parent Too?" *This Emotional Life*, http://www.pbs.org/thisemotionallife/blogs/if-i-had-bad-parents-will-i-be-bad-parent-too.

24 "Parents' Stress Leaves Mark on DNA of Children," University of Wisconsin–Madison's School of Medicine and Public Health website, August 30, 2011, http://www.med.wisc.edu/quarterly/parents-stress-leaves-mark-on-dna-of-children/32279.

25 Brené Brown, *The Gifts of Imperfection* (Center City, MN: Hazelden, 2010), p. 11.

26 Craig Silvey, *Jasper Jones* (New York: Random House, 2009), p. 206.

27 Vivek Wadhwa, "The Leaders of Silicon Valley," *The New York Times*, August 3, 2011.

28 Ken Robinson, *The Element* (New York: Viking, 2009), flap copy.

Index

About the Author

Roma Khetarpal is the founder and CEO of Tools of Growth, through which she helps parents raise kids to "Be Happy, Think Positive, and Do Good." With parenting classes, community outreach, articles, reviews, and blog posts, Tools of Growth provides parents with simple, easy-to-remember, and effective communication tools that can help them build a strong foundation and relationship with their children. By synthesizing the themes and concepts of the personal growth and emotional intelligence fields, along with cutting-edge parenting research, Khetarpal delivers her message in an accessible, reassuring, and personally empowering way.

She is also an Executive Board Member of the Philanthropic Society Los Angeles, which raises funds for Children's Institute, Inc. Khetarpal is working on a line of children's products that will promote self-understanding and emotional intelligence.

Khetarpal also serves on the board of directors at AM-Touch Dental, where she was vice president of sales and marketing for twenty years before founding Tools of Growth, and where she currently teaches quarterly human resource classes. She lives in the Los Angeles area with her husband, Harry. They are the proud parents of two adult children, Nitasha and Navin. Khetarpal enjoys reading, swimming, dancing, cooking, traveling, sunsets and sunrises, oceans, and nature.

Praise for Happy Relaxed Parenting Classes

Tools of Growth with Roma was just what I needed. I have two boys, ages nine and six. The oldest has ADHD, and the younger one does not. I had been having challenges that were only getting worse, not better. I realized my older son was not wanting to open up to me, getting angry with me and wanting to stay away. It broke my heart. I realized I needed to make changes in me. I was searching everywhere, and someone referred me to Roma...one of the best calls I made. I feel like my perspective has changed. I feel happier around my children, and I don't feel like my oldest is pulling away anymore. I was always finding tools for him, but what she taught me works with the whole family.

Thank you for sharing your experiences, challenges, and Tools of Growth.

—*Cheryl B.*

We can't thank you enough for your incredible words and guidance. You made a difference in our understanding of what effective parenting really is.

Thank you so much.

—*Mark C.*

These classes have helped me relax. I realize that when my attitude and demeanor are calm, I receive a positive response as a result. I used to get so worked up from situations with my kids; however I have noticed that they feed off of my energy, and that being a more relaxed parent makes my life, their life, and my husband's life better.

—*Kavita V.*

I generally think my family life is a 9+ out of 10 but, as I've matured, I've realized that I occasionally need to step back and assess my parenting style. The Happy Relaxed Parenting program is a forum that enables me to do that. By discussing my real-world experiences (and those of the other participating parents) in the class setting, I was able to become a more objective witness to how my wife and I are raising our daughters, specifically when the legacy of my own sometimes frustrated and impatient father channels through me.

Roma allowed everyone to participate to their individual comfort level, but by the end of the program I felt like we were all surrogate parents for each other's kids! A very pleasant and rewarding exercise in bettering myself and, hopefully, my daughters.

—*Wes P.*

Roma Khetarpal's Tools of Growth workshop not only inspired me to strive to be a better parent but gave me methods I can use in every interaction with my kids. Once I understood the importance of building emotional intelligence in my children (and myself!) I could focus on "dealing with the feeling" rather than just reacting. I now can use "hot" situations with my kids (and husband!) as a way to focus on solutions in a way where everyone's feelings are valid and explored. I also strive to make every interaction with my kids one of loving expression. I will keep practicing to put meaning into words I want to use, and recognize opportunities to foster feelings of love and support. Thank you, Roma, for the gift of providing tools that enhance my family, help us all grow, and will get passed down to future generations as well!

—*Annette N.*

Roma Khetarpal is a truly inspiring educator. Her classes have taught me essential parenting tools that have helped me become a calmer and happier parent to my three children. Thank you, Roma!

—*Kamila B.*

Thank you for time you spent helping my husband and I learn techniques to "parent honorably." The harmony and satisfaction I feel within my home is amazing. Helping us to understand that parenting does not have to be such a "black and white" standard has been freeing.

Coming from a father who was raised in the military, and then served in the military, left me with a very strict example of parenting. While it makes sense to have clear rules, I was failing to realize that parenting in such a strict manner would not help me achieve my most important goal: raising independent critical thinkers and problem solvers.

We all want the best for our children, and now I have a new "best" to be.

—*Julie C.*

So far, the Happy Relaxed Parenting lessons have been simple and have made a lot of sense. They have also been really easy (for the most part) to apply to my life. Two things have really stood out: (1) when you're happy, you learn better, and (2) try to relate things to what your child (and husband) really wants, which is to relax, play, and have fun.

Thanks so much, Roma, for taking the time to share your knowledge and experience.

—*Elizabeth E.*

Thank you, Roma, for taking the time to help us become happy, relaxed parents! These classes have helped me to really listen and to think feelingly before I communicate. This has helped me at home and in life in general. Although Saira is very young, she feeds off of whatever mood I am in, so I try to remain as positive as possible!

—*Jaya D.*

Roma, it's been an honor to be a part of your classes. I use the information I learn in my personal life as well as my professional life. I often will repeat a lesson or a phrase that I learned from you and pass it on to the other nurses who take my class.

Thanks a million for teaching us how to be mindful of our words, our tone, and our body language. I will continue to aspire to be the best parent I can be.

—*Gina R.*

What I love about your teachings is that it's on a level that anyone can understand. I have learned so much just from our discussions as a group. Kudos to you and your team for all the compassion, dedication, and passion in making our children's world a better place, one insight at a time. I am looking forward to the next year and all of us growing, sharing, and evolving together.

—*Sharmila M.*

You have helped me realize that I have so much parental potential to be the best parent I can be. I truly want to connect with my daughters in a way where they can feel I am always "approachable." I did not have that with my mom and have been secretly fearful that would be the same fate for my girls. Before you came into the equation, I felt I was somewhat on track with developing and maintaining this type of relationship with my girls. I knew there was something missing and there was more I could do but didn't know how to get there. Now I know!

After class yesterday, I came home and discussed our class content with my husband, Dave. He was totally engaged with what I had to say. Wow!! I watched my words and tone so carefully yesterday when I helped Alyssa with her math homework. You would have been proud. It was the best math homework session ever.

—*Tina L.*

This six-week course has made me so much more conscious and mindful of the words that come out of my mouth.

—*Crystal L.*

I have nothing but praise and appreciation for Roma's Tools of Growth. Since being introduced to her work, my relationship with my two young sons has *dramatically* changed from regular frustration and those all-too-often outbursts that leave me feeling guilty, confused, and angry at myself to loving and calm communication. One of the greatest shifts that occurred for me was gaining the awareness that my ultimate desire in parenting my sons was to achieve lifelong intimacy and trust—that closeness that lets them know deep in their soul that they are accepted and understood, and that I would be someone to give them a sense of belonging always. Roma provided the tools that helped me align my thoughts and words with that desire.

Since Tools of Growth, my oldest son began to hug me more and more and would say, "I love you, Mommy" for no apparent reason. My youngest son is less frustrated, and we enjoy our time together more now than before. And for those moments when I see red, Roma has provided some quick and easy tips to calm myself, collect my senses, realign my behavior with my intention, and proceed with a different approach. I have stacks of parenting books and CDs in my library, but I'll reap the dividends of Tools of Growth for a lifetime.

—*Catherine S.*